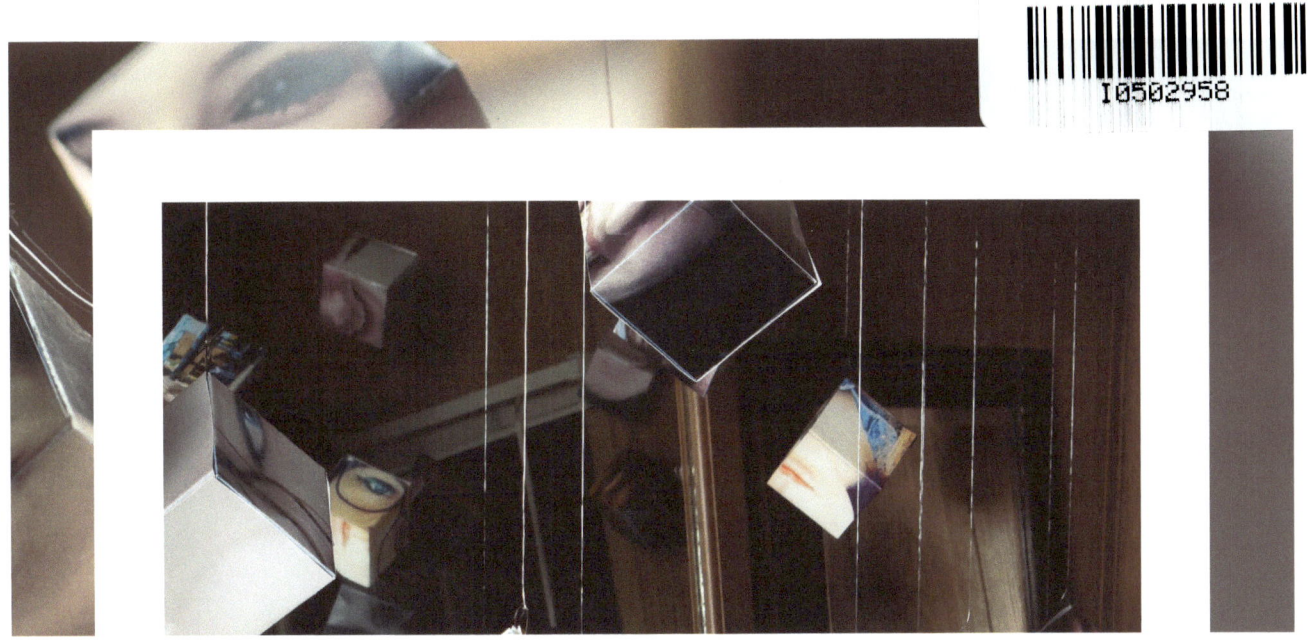

DEEPER (IN)SIGHTS

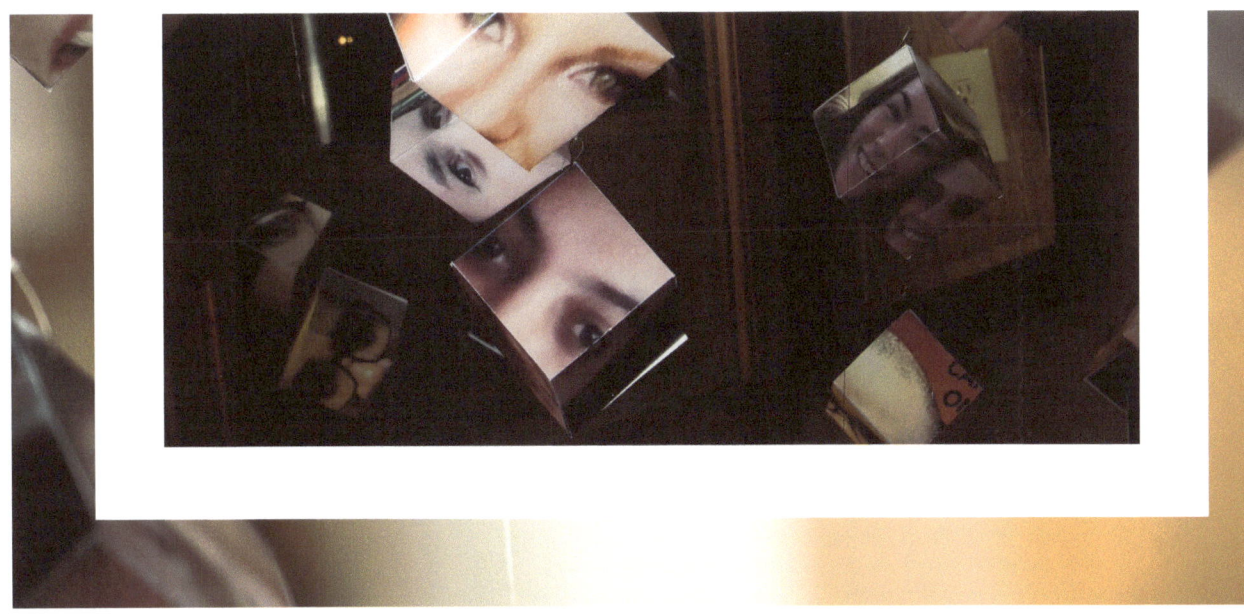

Kimberly A. Redding | Saskia de Rooy

Published by Ten16 Press 2021
ISBN 9781645383079

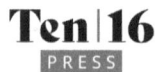

ten16press.com

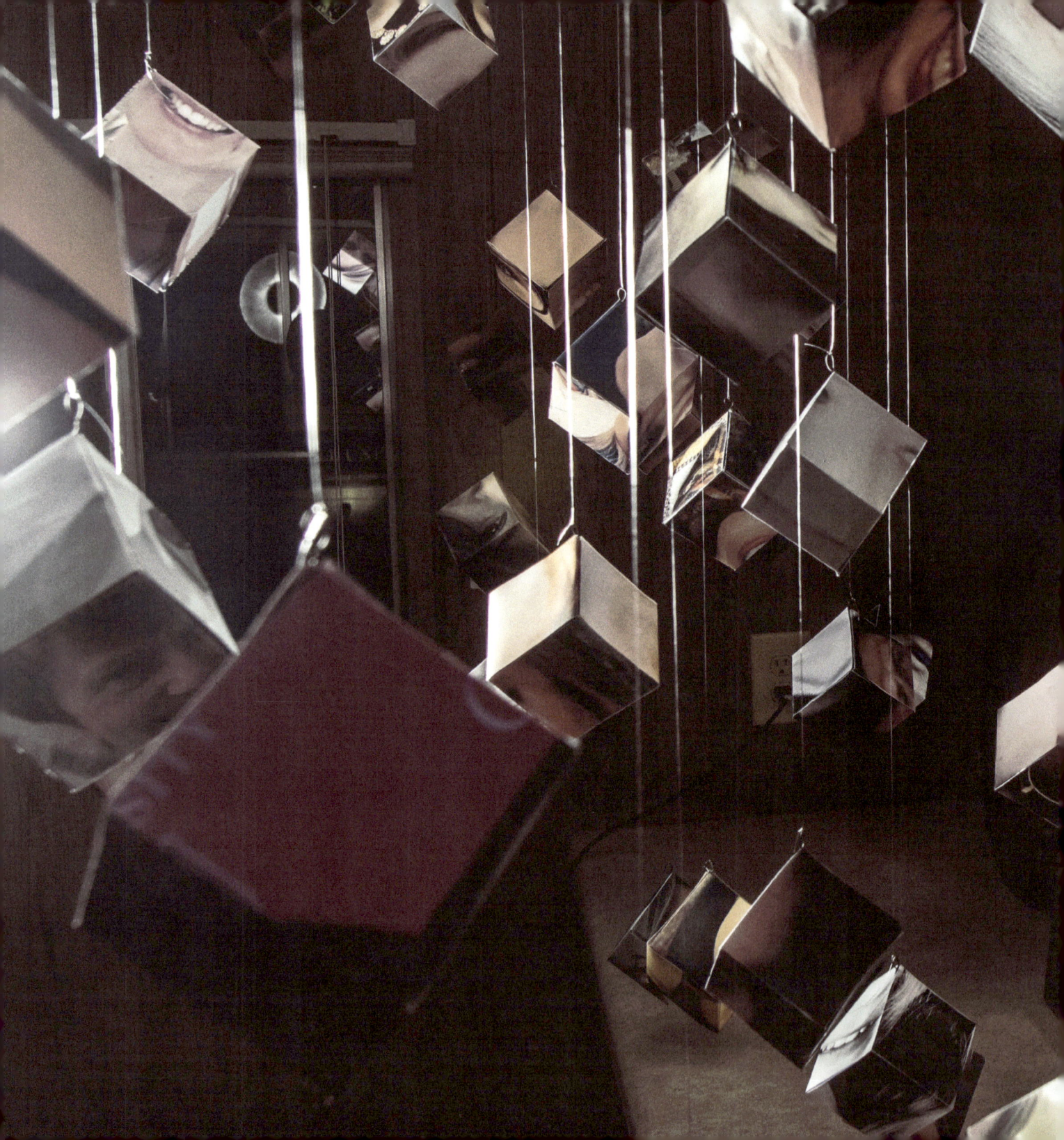

Foreword

As our 2017-18 Artist in Residence, Dutch sculptor Saskia de Rooy led more than 200 members of the Carroll family in an interdisciplinary exploration of identity, community, and humanity. Saskia's ability to engage models and challenge artists inspired Carroll students, faculty, and staff throughout the year. Her boundless curiosity, warm presence, and quick smile also drew in community artists and students from Waukesha South High School and the Waukesha Community Arts Project.

I met Saskia de Rooy in May 2016 at a concert at the *MusiekGebouw,* a world-class concert hall overlooking Amsterdam's waterfront. She was sitting in the row behind us, and she asked me for some of the photos I had taken of her husband, who was one of the musicians. Her card indicated that she was a sculptor, and she said that she would be exhibiting some of her work that weekend on the *Rembrandtplein,* Amsterdam's main square. My spouse and I visited, and we were struck by the evocative beauty of a collection of small sculptural portraits on display. Those portraits sparked a discussion with Saskia about *Poren van Moken,* a multi-artist exhibition of portraits highlighting the diversity and cultural history of the people of Amsterdam.

Saskia and I stayed in touch over the next several months, and our conversations led to the idea that a portrait project at Carroll University could reveal, to each of us and all of us, the richness of individual and collective experience that is the foundation of the Carroll community. I connected Saskia to Amy Cropper, then the chair of Carroll's Department of Visual and Performing Arts. After an initial video conversation, Amy gathered a multi-disciplinary group of faculty to brainstorm with Saskia and develop the contours of a campus-wide initiative.

(in)sight: a portrait project is the product of their collaboration across international and disciplinary boundaries over the next two years. The project galvanized the Carroll community for 18 months, engaging students, staff, and faculty in deep explorations of each other that exploded notions of otherness and emphasized the commonalities that persisted among, and were strengthened by, unique personal and social histories. *(in)sight* was a triumph; it illuminated, challenged, informed, and inspired the Carroll community. I was honored to partake in its magic.

Joanne Passaro
Provost of Carroll University, 2007-2018

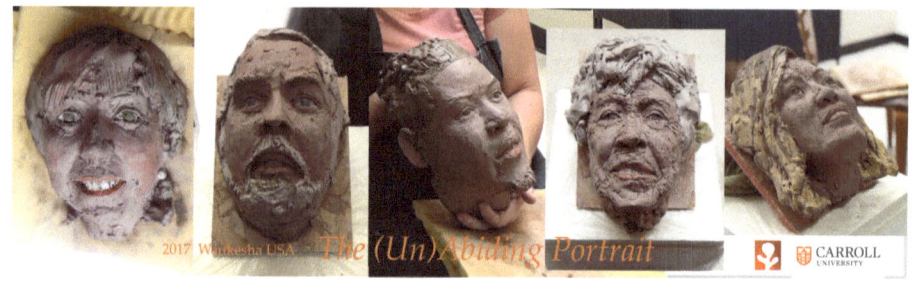

TIMELINE

May 2016

Carroll Provost Joanne Passaro met Dutch sculptor Saskia de Rooy in Amsterdam
Spring 2017 Conversations between Carroll faculty and Saskia generated the idea of an interdisciplinary, community-based exploration of identity and belonging—the core of in(sight): a portrait project.

Sept. 2017

Saskia created the (Un)Abiding Portrait series. For five days, she worked in the Campus Center lobby, sculpting the portrait of a live model while listening to their stories. The next day, that same clay was resculpted into a new portrait. These (Un)Abiding Portraits were—like each of us—unique, temporary, and connected by a common core.

Jan. 2018

Saskia returned to kick off (in)sight: a portrait project, working with Carroll's sculpting, drawing, and painting classes as they began their own portrait projects. Saskia also met with ceramics students at UW-Waukesha (now UWM at Waukesha), Waukesha South High School, and the Waukesha Community Arts Project.

Spring 2018

Models and artists from all corners of Carroll's campus and beyond met one-on-one as the portraits took shape. Students from English, Communication, and History classes interviewed each model using guidelines developed by Kennan Scholarship students. These audio-portraits, like those crafted in the studio, provide a glimpse beneath the surface, a snapshot of an evolving relationship.

April 2018

Faculty and students mounted a public exhibition of portraits, interview excerpts, and cubist-style selfies. We were all invited to see each other's selves in new ways. In the last room, visitors could sit down with a friend—or a stranger—to ask a question, make a sketch, or share a quick game of tic-tac-toe. Each encounter offered new insights into our shared humanity when we, like Saskia, made time to listen and look closely.

Summer 2019

A Pioneer Scholar Grant allowed student Cameron Tom to work alongside history faculty Kimberly A. Redding to transcribe nearly 30 interviews, which offered another chance to listen closely and identify common threads among models. Additionally, the pair used methodological tools drawn from psychology, education, and history to draft essays exploring how individual narratives inform collective and institutional identity.

Saskia & Kimberly met in Amsterdam to plan the book project.

Fall 2019-2020

A manuscript took shape.

Feb. 2021

Orange Hat Publishing accepted (in)sight for their Ten16 Press imprint.

Fall 2021

Carroll University celebrates 175th anniversary.

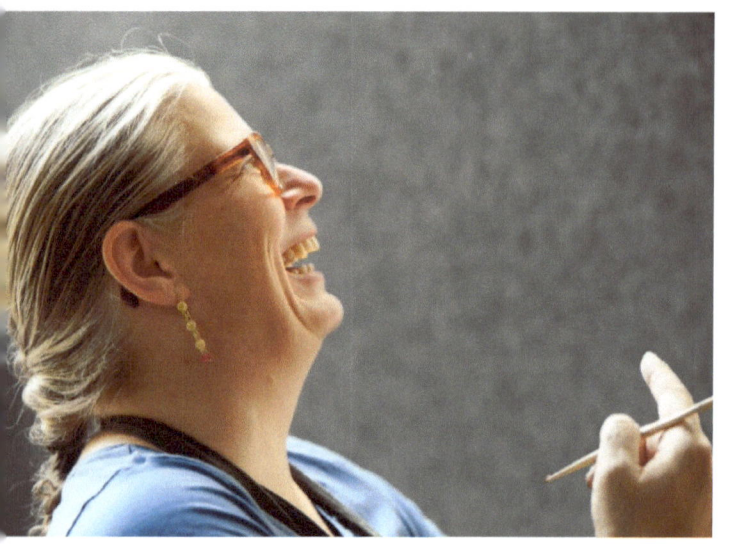

To See One Another Fully

(in)sight: a portrait project was inspired by a community initiative I did in Amsterdam: *Porem van Mokum*—it's Yiddish slang that means "Snapshots of a Beautiful City." When I started *Porem van Mokum* in 2012, I was convinced we can only bridge the gap between Us and Them by looking one another in the eye and being actually interested in one another. With all the challenges ahead of us at this moment, we need all available talents of every available person, no matter their skin color, sex, gender, or background. Belittling or silencing one another will not unearth these talents. Any community, Carroll or any other, deserves and needs the people in it to be able to give their best and to be seen for who they are. You need multiple insights, multiple viewpoints, to get a community into a flow.

Coming to the USA to work on this project, I met so many people, and the names themselves were like messengers from the past—German, Italian, Dutch, English, and Swedish names. They were whispering to me, "My ancestors came from Europe." Having lived in Norway, and traveled in France, Belgium, Germany, Italy, Great Britain, and Poland, I placed the names in their cultures of origin. With each person I met, I saw their forefathers somewhere else in the world. This made it quite hard for me to understand the current aversion to immigration in America (even though we have the same issue in the Netherlands). I come from a family of migrants. Many of my relatives left the Netherlands at one time or another: some for love, some for work, others running from trauma. People leave home for different reasons, but to do so, you have to be courageous. Or desperate. Or traumatized. Or a bit of all three.

Wisconsin reminded me of Norway, with its wooden houses and bright red barns—"oxen red," we call it in Dutch. The plants of the prairie, on the other hand, we only see in garden centres in the Netherlands. Here, they are at home—rooted both literally and figuratively, as are the names of places: Waukesha. Milwaukee, Oconomowoc. They belong here, while other names—Kohler, New Berlin, Fond du Lac—are bedded in European language and history. Coming to the USA was also a strange kind of coming home to a world that is in my living room every day. People talk exactly as they do in the movies we watch at home. I felt I was coming home to the cradle of music I love, while at the same time arriving in an unknown foreign country. The culture seems much the same but *feels* so different.

Walking around this campus, not as a mother, a wife, or a struggling artist— that was freedom. Focusing on work, on teaching, on making the best of this project was sheer joy. Some people on the project team became lasting friends. We tried to teach people to observe, to be honest, to ask questions, to be truly curious. To make the best portrait you possibly can, you have to go deep. It requires persistence, humility, and great respect for the other person. To close or shrink the gaps of mutual misunderstanding or ignorance, you need to be both interested and open. We humans are connected, through history, through our genes, through the terrible things we and our ancestors have done or endured, and through our mutual future. As the Earth herself makes clear, we are all on the same ship. Will we fight one another, capsize, and drown? Or will we learn to see one another fully, to love and to survive?

—*Saskia de Rooy, Carroll University Artist in Residence, 2017-2018*

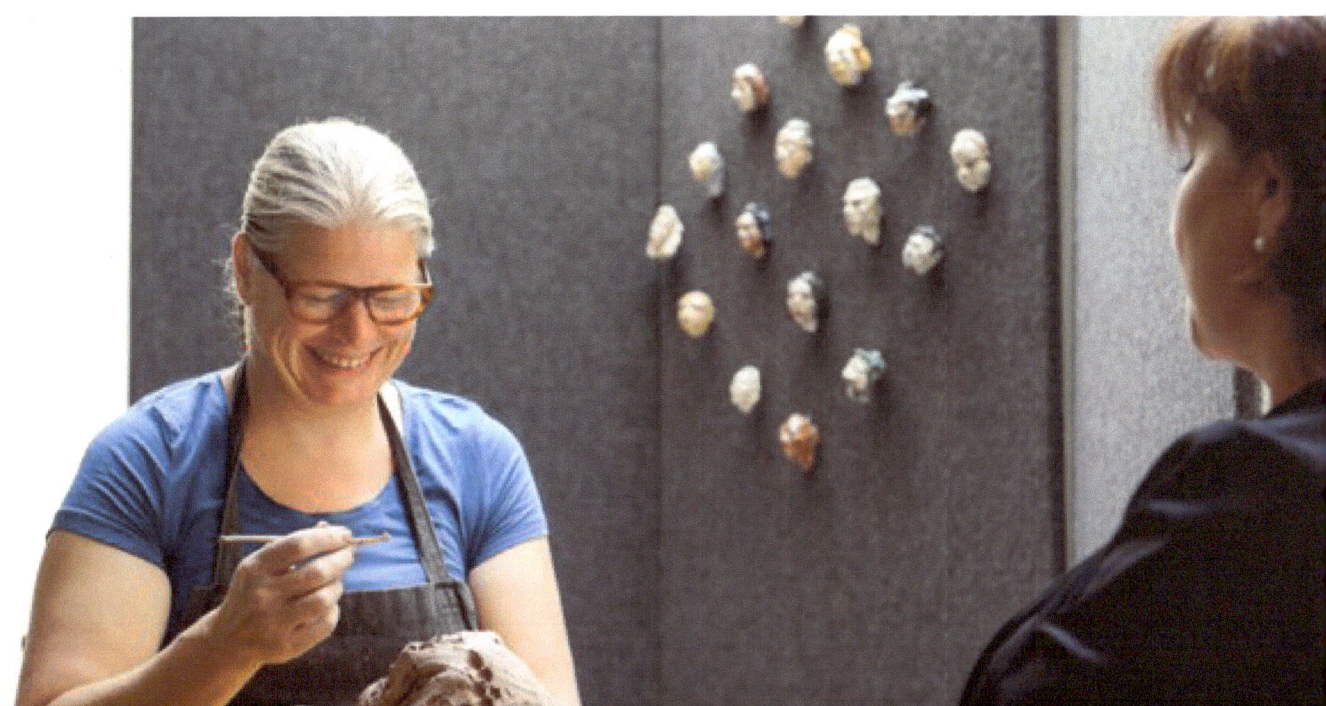

Blurring the Lines

In a sense, the *(in)sight* project started with vulnerability and trust. Saskia didn't know us—I don't think she'd ever heard of Waukesha or Carroll—and we didn't know much about her. But we knew enough to understand that Saskia's creative process is about accepting vulnerability, building trust, and making connections. Could Saskia come to Waukesha and help Carroll University talk to Carroll University? Could she lead students in the making of portraits and conversations? Could she facilitate a large group of students, staff, and faculty to come together around a project that would be as much process and event as individual works of art? Saskia trusted us. We trusted her. She accepted our invitation.

Saskia uses clay and conversation to sculpt ceramic portraits that capture the common humanity in all of us. To watch Saskia make a portrait from a model sitting in front of her is to watch two events unfold simultaneously. Conversation begins quietly and earnestly, back and forth. Each person—artist and model—opening up and beginning to trust the other. The talk gets easier. Lighter. There is usually laughter. The lump of clay in Saskia's lap also evolves; rough features emerge, then distinctive details. When the process is over, the two people smile and gaze together at the finished sculpture. Where there was a lump of clay and two strangers, there is now a new sculpture and a new relationship.

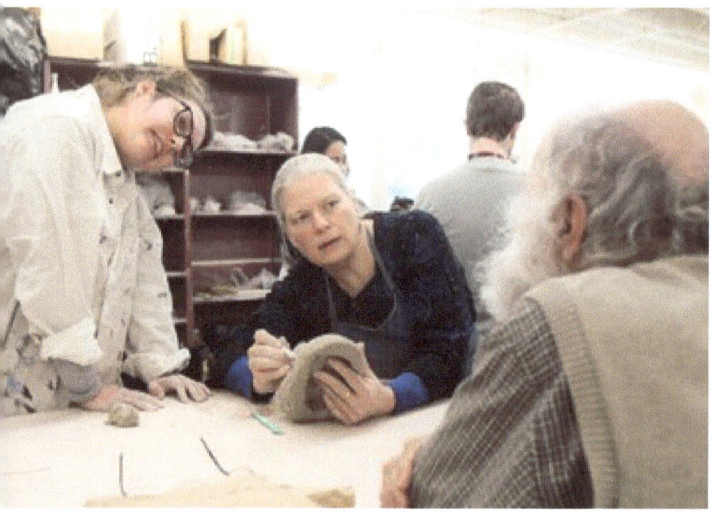

At times, *(in)sight* involved as many as 20 student artists (beginners to advanced) and 20 models all in the same room. Making art for—and in—public spaces infuses the creative process into everyday activities—working, talking, taking a phone call, waiting for something else to start or end. And in that context, in the midst of life and art-making, the conversations flowed. I heard students laughing with their staff or faculty models. Nervous artists (often students taking their first college art class) were put at ease by a question from their model about family. As in Saskia's own portrait-making practice, the lines began to blur between the creation of a portrait and the creation of a friendship.

Like Saskia, I believe in blurring the lines between art and life, in bringing the creative process into our day-to-day lives, where it can engage people in unexpected ways. Over the course of our year-long collaboration, the *(in)sight* project did just that. We talked to people we had never met, and we discovered commonalities that had been there all along. How fortunate that a chance encounter at an Amsterdam concert hall led Saskia de Rooy to Carroll University in Waukesha. How fortunate that now, along with so many others on this campus, I call Saskia a friend.

—Amy Cropper, Professor of Art, Carroll University

Elaine Yarger

Just see what happens

Interviewed by Morgan Levene and Steven Grabowski, nominated anonymously

When I applied for colleges… I didn't know what I wanted to do. I kind of had an idea of what I wanted from a college, and then I went to Carroll's open house. It's funny because I met two of my best friends there. And then I got in the car with my parents, and they were like, "Well, where do you want to go?" I was like, "I guess Carroll. I don't know." And then Carroll gave me a scholarship, so that made it work. So I was like, "All right, let's try it." The other reason was the study abroad because I wanted to do that. So I went to Ireland for a semester. I was in Maynooth, right outside Dublin for the whole semester. I met some really good friends. I got to study more Irish history, and… you know, it worked.

Carroll was just kind of a gut feeling more than anything. But it worked out. I met my boyfriend; I met all my friends. I met the professors… and I'm still alive. Carroll's not really known for history, but our department is really good and… what I realize now, is that's what I was looking for. I didn't know it then because I was 18. I didn't know anything; I didn't really know anything. I literally… When I was very young, originally, I wanted to be a paleontologist. I loved dinosaurs. I think I could find bones. I think I'm talented enough to do that. And then in middle school, I had to do a project looking up a career we wanted to do. I was watching a lot of Criminal Minds, so I said I want to do FBI. I don't know why. I don't want to do that at all. And in high school, I felt like, "I don't know anything. I don't know who I am. I'm just here hanging out." And I kind of just fell into wanting to work in museums. I was like, "I'm good at history. I like history. Let's just see." And then now I'm here. So it was… not very driven, more of " Let's see what I like. We'll hope for the best." And it worked out, you know.

My regrets? That's a good Q. I don't really think I have that many regrets. This is a lame answer, I do admit, I don't… I don't have anything I would do differently, mainly because every single thing that's happened to me, it makes me who I am. They're my experiences. Some of them give me really good jokes. Maybe the one thing I would do differently would maybe… just be nicer to my younger self…

But I followed my train. Now we're here. And medieval history—she's got me. The cool thing about the medieval period is that the mindset was, "Does this work, yes or no?" They would just do things that work. You don't have to fully understand everything about it for it to work. That's my vibe: It works. We don't need to know everything about it. If it ain't broke, don't fix it, you know? The other really fun part of history is asking "Why does opinion change? Why? What happened to change the thinking?" Because there's always something. Maybe somebody messed up. Take anti- Catholicism in England after the Reformation: you have this idea they're all thinking "Pope's going to kill us," basically, when really, most everyone thought "I don't think they are." But one dude, Titus Oates, he said, "What if I wrote a book that said Catholics are to come kill us? Let's just see what happens."

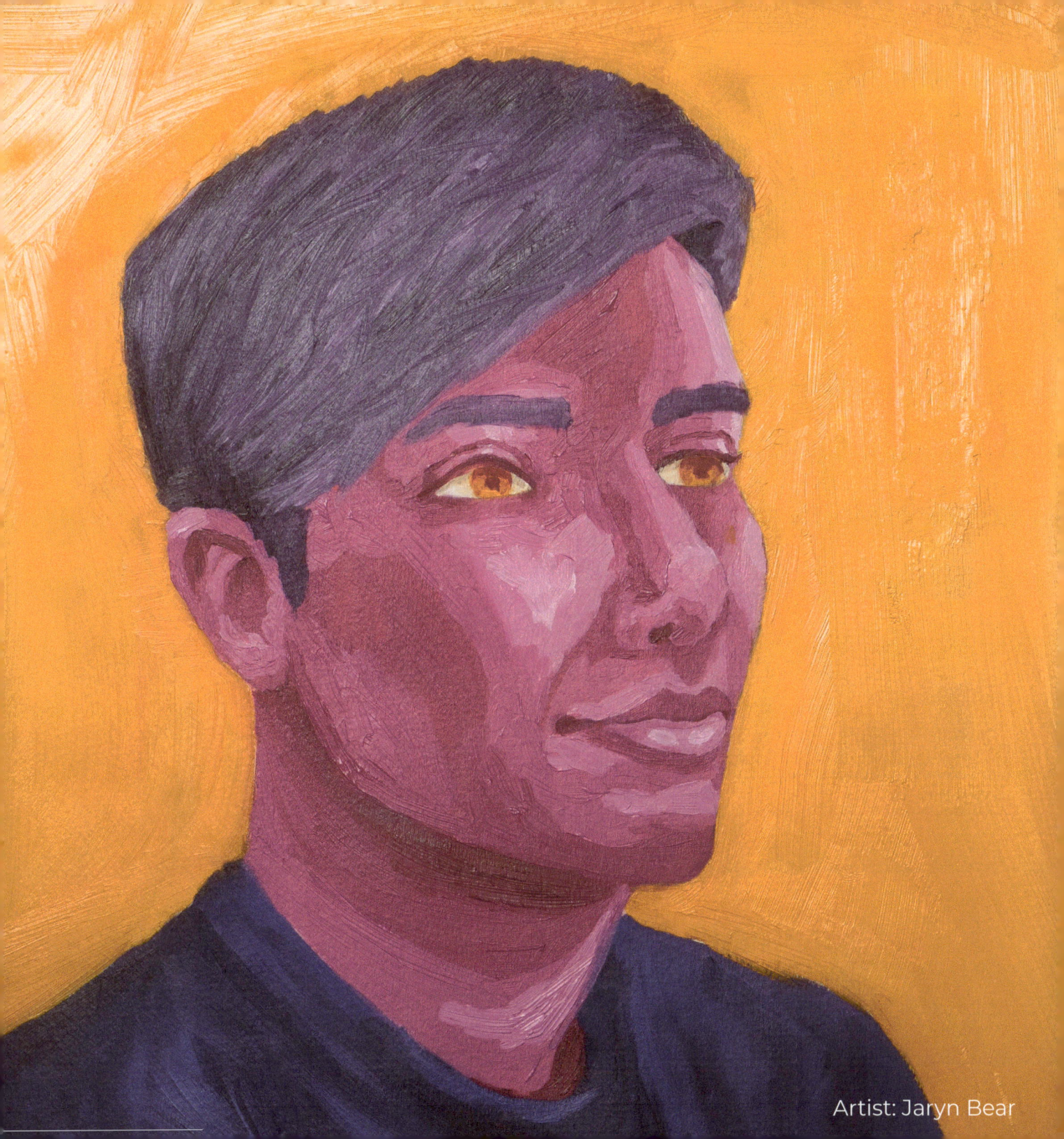

Artist: Jaryn Bear

Isabelle Banke

Invisible scars

Interviewed by Katie Dobrzynski, nominated anonymously

I have a connective tissue disease called Loeys-Dietz syndrome. I had an aneurysm in my ascending aorta, which is the main blood vessel that comes out of your heart. I've had it—I *had* it from the time I was born… until last summer when I had open-heart surgery and had my entire ascending aorta replaced. So [all my life] I couldn't do anything where I might get hit in the chest. I pretty much eliminated contact sports. I tried gymnastics; I was way too tall. I tried golf, no. So I started riding when I was eight… and horses were my first love. When I was ten, my mom said, "You can't just have one hobby; pick something else." … I picked drums. In high school, I did concert band, percussion ensemble, jazz band, and drumline. Drumline is still my favorite, so for the last year and a half, I've been working super hard to get a marching band and drumline here. Most of our band is volunteers like me—I'm an athletic training pre-med major. I don't have any reason to be in band other than that I like it. I'd go insane if… you need *something*, you know what I mean? If my whole life revolved around school and studying and the other stuff I do, I think I'd lose it.

I want to be a connective tissue specialist. I'd like to help people through their crisis point. I think before surgery I was afraid—because of the course load, how hard it is to get into med school and then your residency and fellowship, and blah, blah, blah. But open-heart surgery—I proved to myself that I can pretty much do anything because I survived that. People think that I live a really hard life with these limitations, but really, the hardest part was having to explain it to people because I look fine; nothing looks wrong with me. Especially *before* I had surgery, and I couldn't just pull off my shirt and say, "Look, there's a giant scar there." It's huge. You can't miss it.

I wrote this paper my freshman year: "Invisible Scars." I knew the surgery was coming, and I knew that inside me was messed up. But I couldn't *show* anybody. The whole underlying theme was looking normal but actually *being* different. Appearances tell you I'm just a normal, tall blonde. You know. Another one of *those*. But if you know what my life has been like, I'm actually so very different…

College is weird because I have so many new friends, and you're so close to them, but then they say, "Hey guys, look. I brought my brother for Siblings' Weekend," and you think, "You have a brother?!?" I'm consciously aware that I'm probably not like most kids here, but… I feel like I wear the black sheep costume more than other people see it on me…

I've had to do a lot of coming to terms with stuff; after surgery I had to ask for so much help… And I'm not dating anymore, because the guy I was dating at the time, when I was finally feeling good enough—over a month after surgery—he said, "We should go to a steakhouse." But he didn't anticipate I couldn't cut my own steak. He had to sit there and cut my steak for me, and the waiter gave us such weird looks. You can get embarrassed about it, or you can embrace it because you can't control it. Honestly, it's just like, "Ok, here I am. This is what I'm dealing with. Take it or leave it." I realized that being different is actually my strength. And that's everyone's strength.

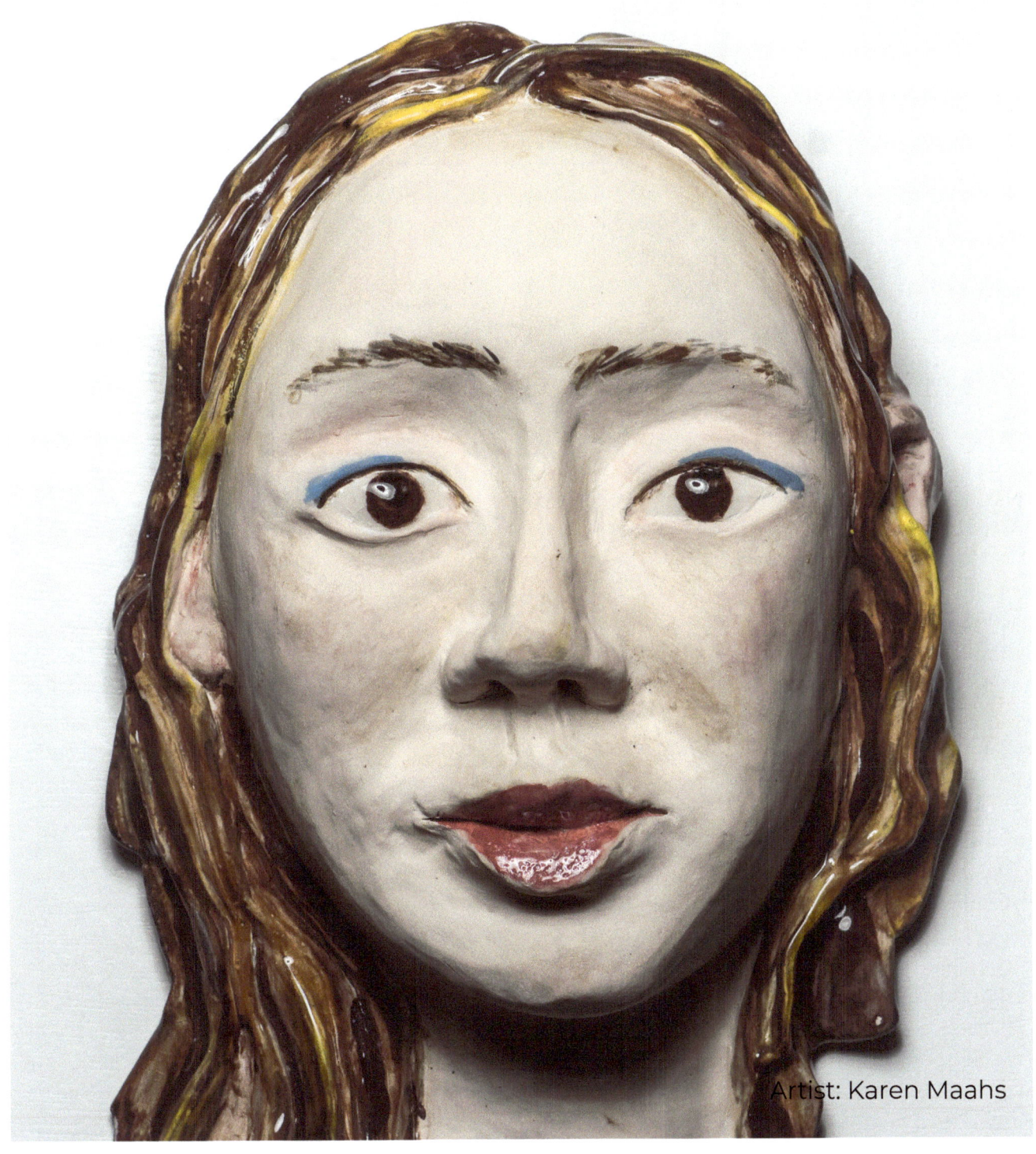

Artist: Karen Maahs

Zach Staszewski

Alumni for life

Interviewed by Claire Pomey and Erin Sullivan, nominated by Sara Meyer

I graduated from high school in 2007 and started at Carroll College. And then after my freshman year, they officially changed to Carroll University. So I technically went to both, which is pretty cool. Only a few graduates that can say that, and I feel affinity towards both. I get it when alumni totally affiliate with Carroll College, but I also see where the University has gone, and so it's been exciting to be a part of that. I was super involved when I was a student. I was an R.A., Student Senator, Orientation Mentor, in the theater and the choirs, and I wanted to find a career where I can blend that.

I enjoy innovating and then seeing stuff come to fruition… I think it's helpful that I'm an alum because I'm also creating events for my friends sometimes, too. I run the Young Alumni event series. I'm still in that category, so when I'm reaching out, it's like "You better come to this event because it's gonna be fun," and they usually do. That was what I did while I was here as well. I worked in Student Activities, on Student Senate I planned events, for the RAs I was a social coordinator, and so on. That history just evolved into what I do now, which is great…

I'm patronized a little bit [at work] because I'm the loud one with energy. Sometimes the more senior people in our office can find me overwhelming. But I think they appreciate it, too. They'll say, "We laugh more since you've gotten here." *At* me? Behind my back? Or all together as a group laughing? I feel like we're all together. We have a month-long initiative throughout the entire country that engages Carroll community members to address hunger-related issues, whether in Milwaukee and Waukesha or in their communities. We also have some options on campus; you'll see us sorting food in the Campus Center. We send out postcards to something like 23,000 people, and all we want to do is hear back from them, whether they volunteer or drop off a bag of groceries at a local food pantry. We just want to know that they're getting engaged in hunger-related issues. And then we can say, "Hey, we raised the equivalent, as a Carroll community, of 50,000 meals in one month in 33 states across the country."

It's just about leaving things better than I found it, building initiatives, or developing processes that work better or connect us, or make it a more valuable experience. It's challenged me in a lot of good ways and using everything I've learned. I just want people—I don't need to hear this recognition or get it personally—but I want to know that people think Carroll's doing a good job… I just want people to have the same feeling towards Carroll as I have, as an alumnus. I want them to have good memories of the University, of their classmates, and of the people that they met here, and to know that Carroll can continue to support them socially and professionally as they move on. We've got an unofficial motto: You're a student for four years, but you're alumni forever. Someone gave me the statistics when I first started; I think about 80% of our alumni have graduated since 1985. And we have people who are celebrating their 75th class reunions. No matter what you're doing, where you are, what your family or your job situation is, you'll always be a graduate of Carroll. I want people to feel pride in that.

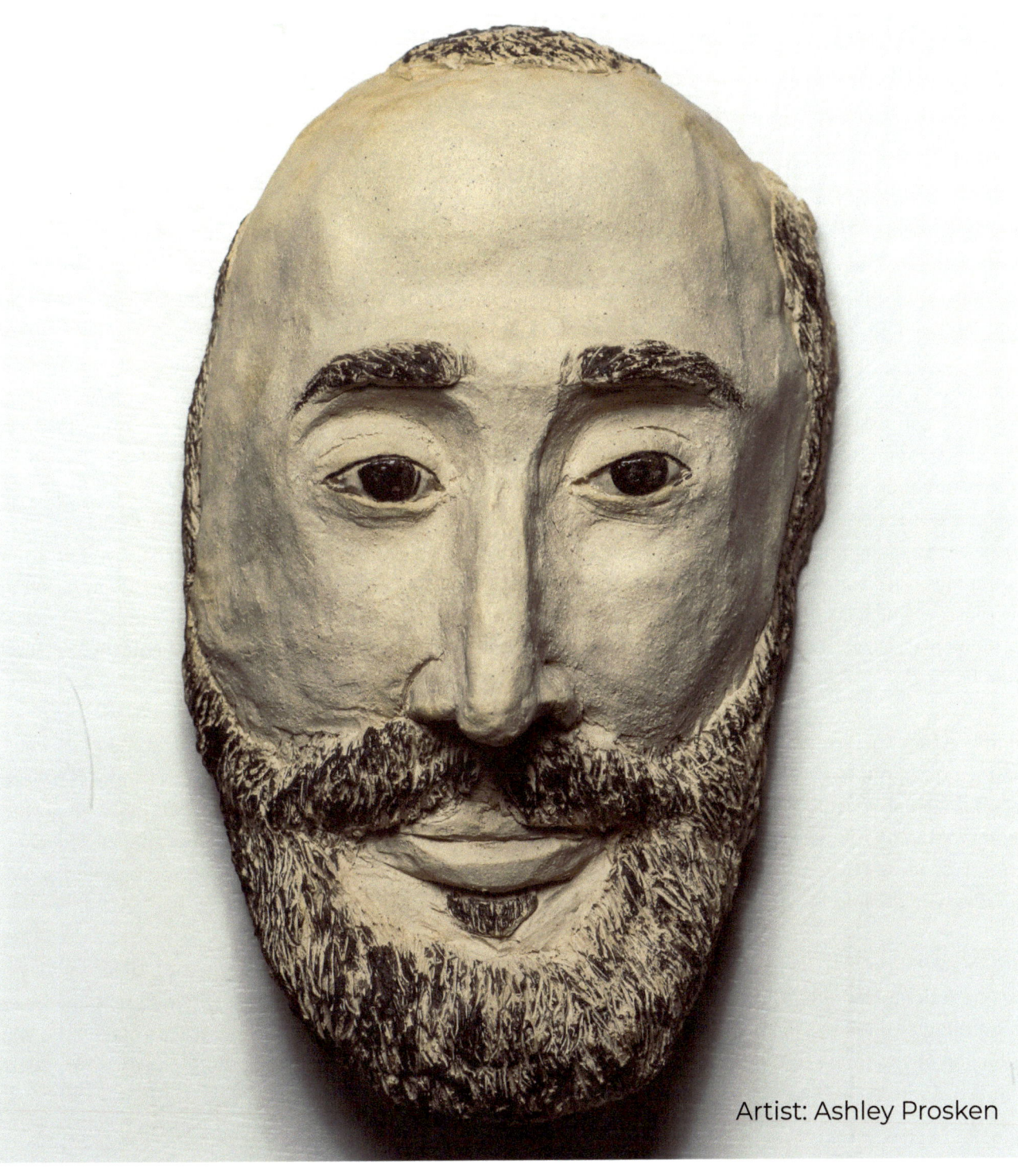

Artist: Ashley Prosken

Steph Kilen

Taking time

Interviewed by Saskia de Rooy, nominated anonymously

I'm a storyteller. And so you know, everything revolves around my being able to write stories and share stories and listen to people, people's stories. If we slow down, we find similarities in people's stories. But because life now, particularly with social media, is just snapshots of what we decide to show… I think we miss that a lot these days. My undergrad degree is in journalism, and I started teaching right around the time when fake news was starting to become a real thing, and people were sharing all kinds of things. So the basic writing class ended up being a lot more about media literacy. And it was amazing to see what students understood at the beginning, and then to see them start to think and disseminate information for themselves.

One of the things that's most interesting about this *(in)sight* project is that all of it is about taking time: doing the art, looking at a person in a new way, having the conversations as you're doing it, doing these interviews, and seeing someone first as a full person—and then as a student, teacher, artist, or whatever it is. People are much more than a snapshot or a caption. That's probably an important aspect of my portrait.

There are so many ways of telling stories. Sometimes they—the art and the actual words—go hand in hand, and sometimes… It's sort of funny because the insight portrait looks like me, but it doesn't. The student didn't do my glasses, which is completely understandable. But I wear them all the time, so… well, my image of myself includes glasses, so that was sort of strange. But right away, my husband said, "Oh, that's your nose." That's what he saw.

At the first sitting, I remember you showing all the different ways people have done portraits, some of the really abstract ones. And I remember seeing all of the portraits at the end; they were nearly all literal, more representational than abstract. I think that… that is somewhat along the lines of what I saw in my students. They were very afraid to try things. Part of that is, you know, about the grade: "I have to get a good grade, and I have to do well because I have to get a good job. I have to follow these rules because that's how you succeed in life." But it was interesting because where those rules come from is sort of arbitrary.

I try to ask things like, "Well, what if it's a different thing? What if there's a different rule or a different way to go about doing something?" That brings an opportunity to have a conversation on a very different level. And those things sometimes have to simmer. They have to be planted before they bloom because maybe the situation, the environment isn't right in that moment for them to bloom. But if they're *in* there, the ideas are ready to make a difference when they're needed.

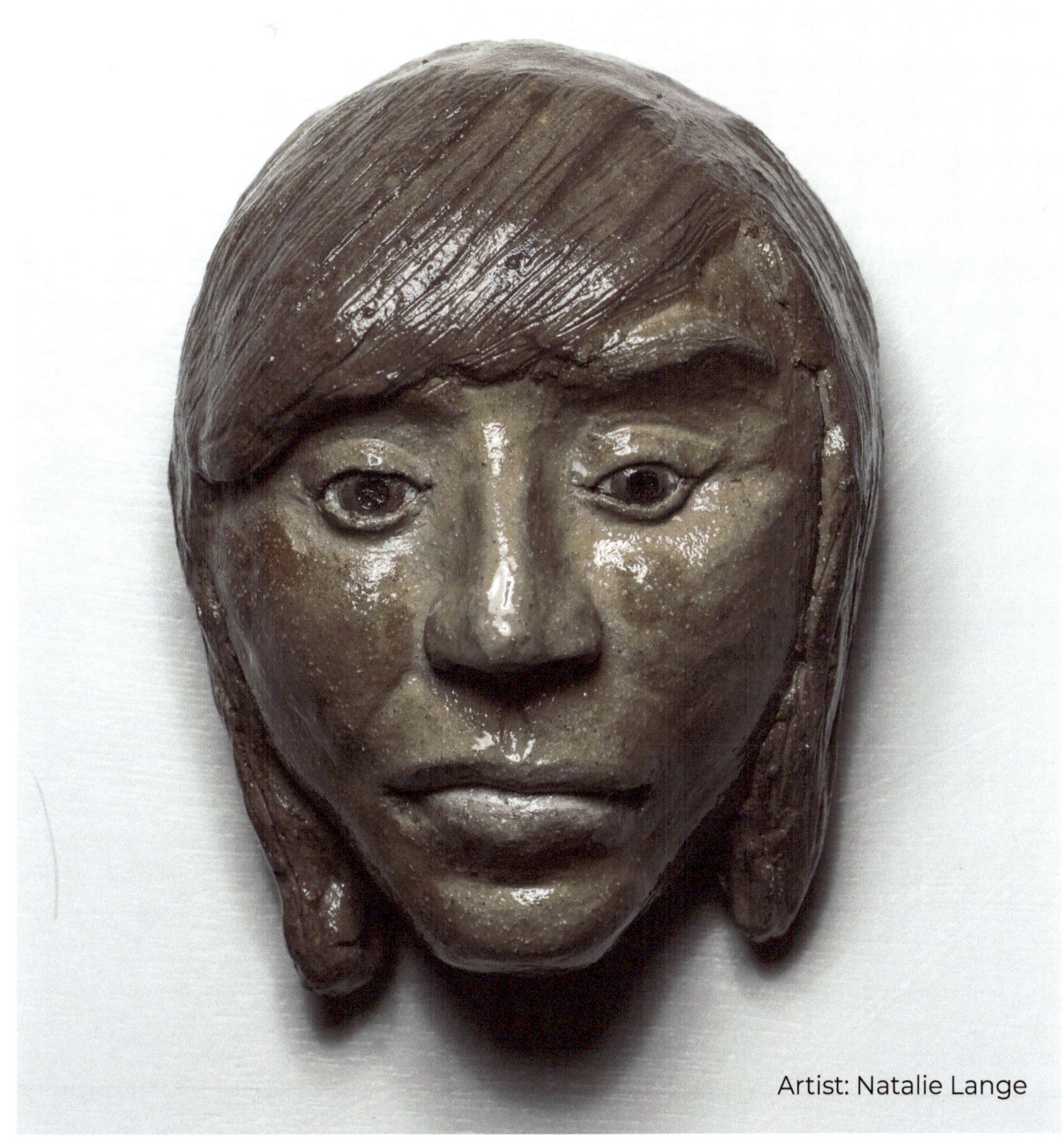

Artist: Natalie Lange

Megan Baker

Kindred spirits

Interviewed by Makenzie Ferguson and Steven Grabowski, nominated by Sara Meyer

I grew up being really, really close to my family. I'm from a rural area up in north central Wisconsin. So I grew up close to friends, family, and extended family, and having that support system. Those lessons: Work hard. We have your back. We're proud of you. We see the things that you're doing. That's really important when you're really trying to figure yourself out after college, navigating the adult world. My grandmothers are both wonderful, and my mom is such a hard worker as well. So I carry a lot of that with me.

I went to a large state school, and being from a small rural town, I felt completely drowned and overwhelmed by all of the choices. There were more students on that one campus than there were in about twelve towns put together at home; it was very overwhelming for me. And trying to navigate the culture shock as well, coming to a city where there's a lot of wealth. I come from an area where there's not a lot of wealth. People work really hard. They work themselves to the bone, long hours, long shifts just to survive. So having classmates coming from very well-to-do families and having more opportunities, it was intimidating, really—competing for spaces in any kind of organization or trip or anything like that... I know—it's all part of the growing experience, and you really do have to be resilient and succeed with... despite the obstacles that people really don't, or really can't, see. So even though my job is advising and coordinating international programs, when there's a rural, first generation student... Those are my kindred spirits because I get how scary the process is.

I also teach transfer students—of any age group, any kind of background... Last semester was a really great experience, really wonderful discussions. I make the point to make sure that everybody learns about each other and how much cultural variety people bring into the workplace, the school place, the classroom, I should say... We all have had life obstacles. People, as soon as they really started trusting the class, they opened up, and they talked more about their, you know, things that have happened in their lives that have really shaped them. Some of them obstacles, some of them opportunities...

Usually you can get a good read on a student based on the energy that they bring in. If they are just super determined to go out there and do the things that they want. That is... That's a different support system for me from a student who is just really not sure. It's taken a lot of practice to be able to move in and out of those different energies that students bring in, because we have to meet students where they're at.

Generation Z students give me a lot of hope too—just how kind they are, how understanding that they are towards one another. The empathy and compassion is something that I haven't seen in a lot of people. Not that I have a ton of experience with every single person and culture. But, you know, I can tell from just my five, going on six years in International Advising at Carroll: empathy and patience is something that Generation Z has embodied.

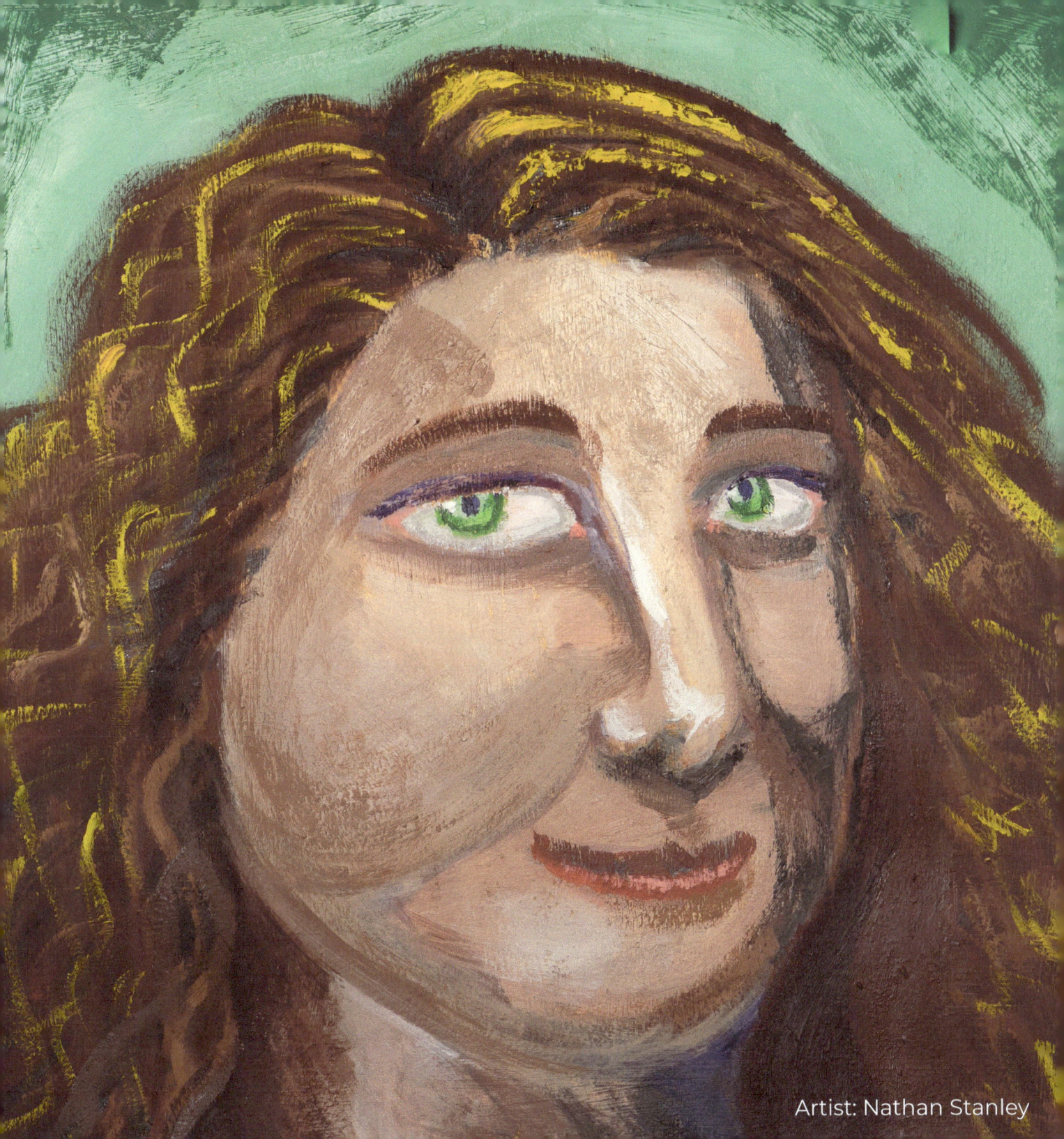

Artist: Nathan Stanley

Jon Gordan

Not a perfect science

Interviewed by Ashley Labodda, nominated by Amy Cropper

I teach Interpersonal Communication, and Intercultural, and even Communication Technology in Society. In all these courses, we look at what makes relationships work or not work. How do people express themselves? Will they be effective? Ineffective? I've always been more of a person watcher as opposed to an interacter, and studying communication allows me to do that. I think, "Ok, what are you communicating by the way you're sitting there?"

I'd never been out of the States, but at my undergraduate college, most people did study abroad. I went to Egypt because I was learning Arabic… You get dropped off in a foreign country; you either adapt or get on the next plane going home. You're standing there, thinking, "Mom? Dad? Can you help me?" but Mom and Dad aren't there anymore. I mean they're *there*, but a long way away. And it's like, "Well, can I do this?" We all have those self-doubts. You have to convince yourself to give it a try and see what happens. When I got off the plane in Egypt, there was supposed to be a representative from the university to pick me up. [No one came]. Who do I call? How do I… I don't even know where the phones are!

You come back with so much more self-confidence because you survived, you got through culture shock. I remember being in Egypt; I was crushed after about the second week. I was sick of the food. I was physically ill. I just want to go home. I missed my girlfriend. I even went and changed my return flight so I could come back earlier. Then after I stayed another couple months and sort of adapted, I got more confidence. There were so many things I wanted to do, so I went back and extended my stay so I could go down to Karnak and other places. That was the biggest thing for me; you *think* you can do things, but you never realized that you'd never had to do them *on your own*. Now you do, and odds are you'll succeed. At that point you're like, "Hey, I'm pretty tough."

Being Caucasian, you don't realize the benefits; it's just part of life. Even in Egypt I, blended in enough; at the time, I had a thick beard and long curly hair, so they assumed I was Egyptian. But I went to Japan—the most wonderful, kind people you'll ever meet—but you get those looks every now and again, especially from kids. They were either fascinated, or… you just got treated a little bit differently, and you wonder, "Well, what are minorities treated like in *this* country?" What little things happen that you just never think really happen?

Don't let things outside of your control stay with you. Yeah, you're going to get upset. That's natural. But don't hold it in; just let it become a part of you, just let it go. It's your life. If you meet somebody and they're mean, just avoid them, get them out of your life, and go on… I gave up a good job and went to another job. It didn't work out. At first I was very upset; how could they do this to me? But then right afterwards: there's a reason this is happening, something better is going to come along. And here I am, and this is better. It's an improvement. I'm quite happy with it. My whole life has been with people roughly 20 years old. I know older generations say, "Oh, Millennials. They don't get it…" I say, "They're not that much different, really. If anything, they're an improvement."

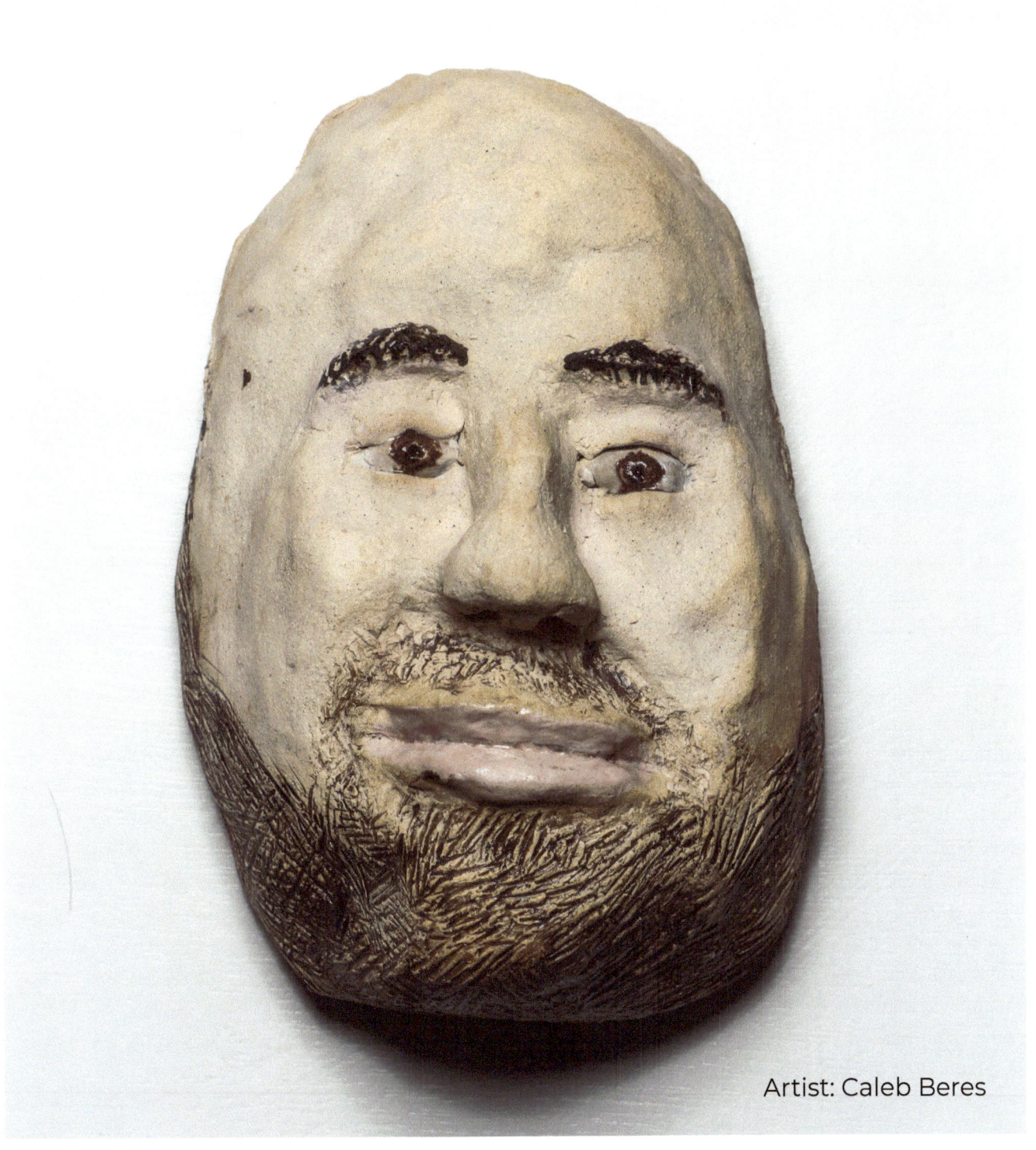

Artist: Caleb Beres

Jocelyn Guzman
Just keep going

Interviewed by Kylie Peters, nominated by Amy Cropper

I don't partake too much in Carroll stuff. My work in facilities, to be quite honest, is not that exciting. I generally just listen to complaints all day... It's nice and perks up my day when somebody calls and says, "Hey, the guys really did great!" or "You know, they clean up really well." It's... it's a job...Not to say it's a bad job. You get to meet good people. There are some really good people to work with, and the community is pretty good. But it's not necessarily–they always preach about finding your passion, and this is not really my passion...

I love music. I can't be without music. I even work with music playing. I don't know if it has to do with my up-bringing. My dad used to be a professional DJ. My mom sang in church and all that... I did musicals in high school. I enjoy the idea of being a different person. I loved playing Cha Cha from *Grease*. She was so opposite from me. I'm so reserved, and out there I'm flaunting myself. We had rehearsed that big dance scene between Cha Cha and Danny Zucko. He has to grab me by the waist and basically flip me. We'd rehearsed it multiple times. In the second to last show, he almost dropped me. I hit the floor; my knees hit and it *hurt*. The entire audience could hear the boom. I wanted to laugh, but we're in the middle of the show. You've just got to keep going. Just get up, keep going, just keep going… You can't let something derail you. There's always going to be something to sidetrack you. Always something, an obstacle... But if that holds you back, well, how are we ever going to get anything done?

...It's so satisfying when you get together with a group of people [with] one goal in mind, and you accomplish it. It's the most satisfying feeling: "We did that." Even through disagreements… You have an obstacle, you over-come, and you figure it out. You come up with a solution. ...I think a lot of people don't realize my anxiety and depression affects me every single day. I try to be in control of it, but... it's just a reminder that you don't know what anybody is going through. I know that there have been times where people have come across me on a day when I'm just really struggling to keep myself together, and I may come off as very blunt or very hard when I'm not trying to be. I've had some people say "Wow. She just has a bad attitude," or "Wow. She just looks like she's not approachable." You never know what someone's going through. You never know. So just don't take a person at face value… "So-and-so said you looked really mean." I'm not. I can talk to somebody and open up. I'd like to. I like to talk; I'll talk for hours about musical theatre, bringing up my favorite shows. So when I hear that somebody thinks I'm mean [or] have a bad attitude, it bothers me a bit. Don't let that outward appearance always give that first impression… I am a nice person. I am an approachable person. I'm just incredibly shy. I have really bad anxiety. I think that's the biggest thing that bothers me.

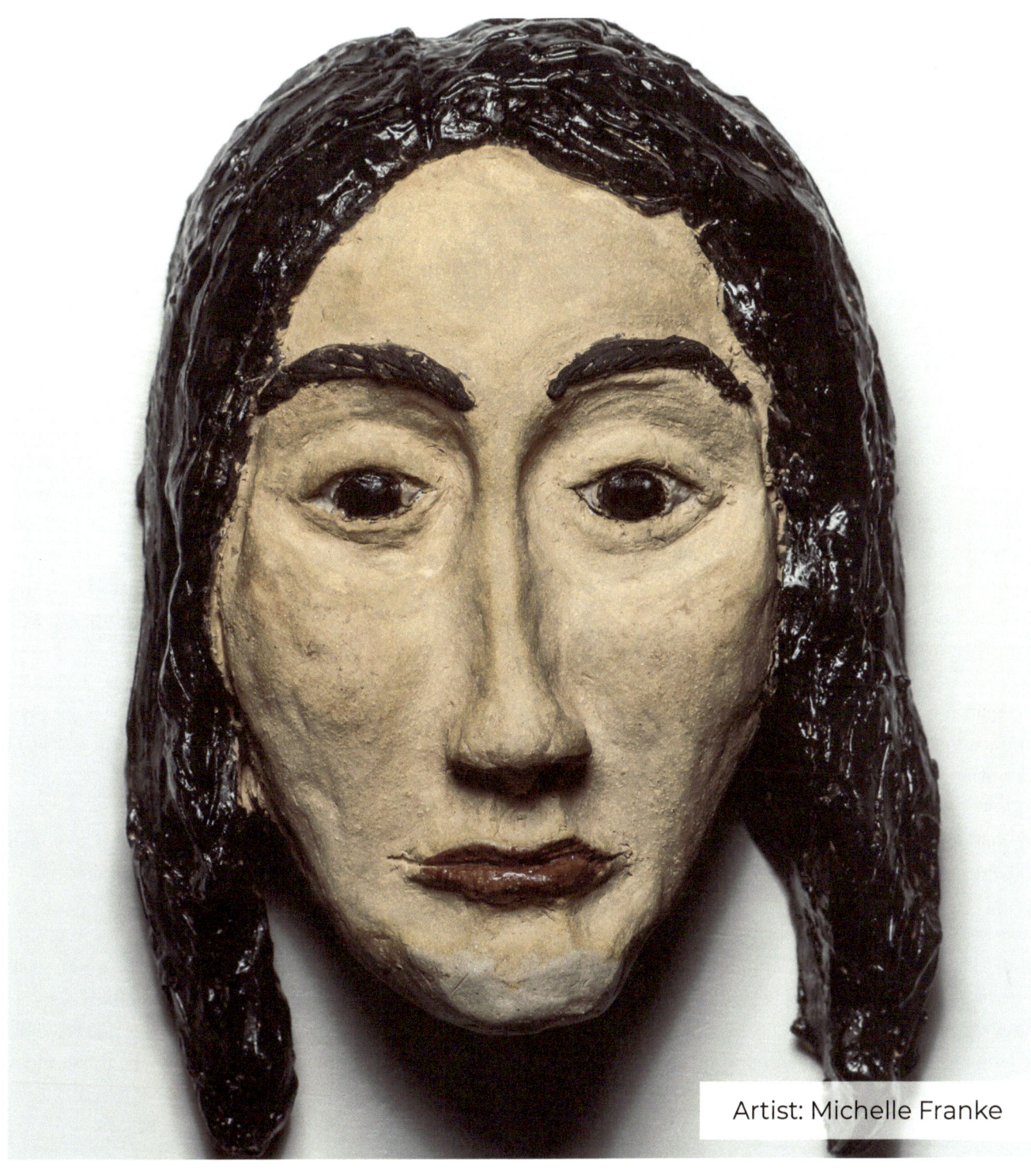
Artist: Michelle Franke

Carl Ervin
A better future today

Interviewed by Amanda Elkins and Kayla Geissberger, nominated by Amy Cropper

I really enjoy science fiction. I'm a big sci-fi fan, and I just love Captain Kirk. He's different in the sense that he'll try things that are outrageous, outside the box. And I like that. He was very creative, just a little bit outrageous, and always tried something off the wall. It's clever. He may not have been the smartest or the strongest, but he found a way to win. The script writers were really good, and I could picture that. So when I have to deal with situations, I think, "OK. What's another way of looking at it? It doesn't have to be straightforward. It can be an alternative way. I guess [Captain Kirk] also influences my work in that I try not to take things too seriously. You still have to take it seriously, and do the best that you can, but also have a little fun with it. And I'm passionate about trying different things. The biggest risk I've taken was moving up here to Wisconsin. Another risk I just took was travelling outside the country. I'm like Kirk, but I'm not a risk-taker as much as I'd like to be.

The most important person in my life is my mom; the reason being that she taught me about values. She always looks for the good in folks and taught me God first, then family, and to be positive. She's always helping other folks, and I try to follow in her footsteps. She was also an example in the sense of peace she had. When you grow up seeing things like this, you say, "Well, that's how they're supposed to be." From day one. That's how you remember where you're going. [The happiest moment of my life] was when I was fully accepted into the church because that's when you see that... your purpose in life is more than just you. It's about giving yourself over to something much greater.

No matter how difficult things are, it'll pass. You can move forward. Look past the troubles. Look for the opportunities in the future because it can be better. Do not let the troubles be an anchor holding you down. This is something I'm still working on: not letting the past stop me from having a better future today.

My dad always taught me to always give your best, to work hard. Even if you're not feeling the best, you just push through it, and you go to work; if you're tired or sick, [you] can still make it. [He's] sort of my role model, too.

I like seeing a student get that "aha" moment. It's like "Hey, I didn't think I could get through this, so I didn't think that I'd continue at Carroll," and then you're putting him in the right direction or helping him... You see him walk across the stage [and think] "Wow. You got your degree. You could do this." I've tried to go a little bit above and beyond. If there's a way to help people because it's not about me; it's about how you can help other people realize their dreams. I mean, someone said, "A life well-lived..." That's what I want to do. If you can make the world a little bit better than it was through your passing through it, then you led a successful life.

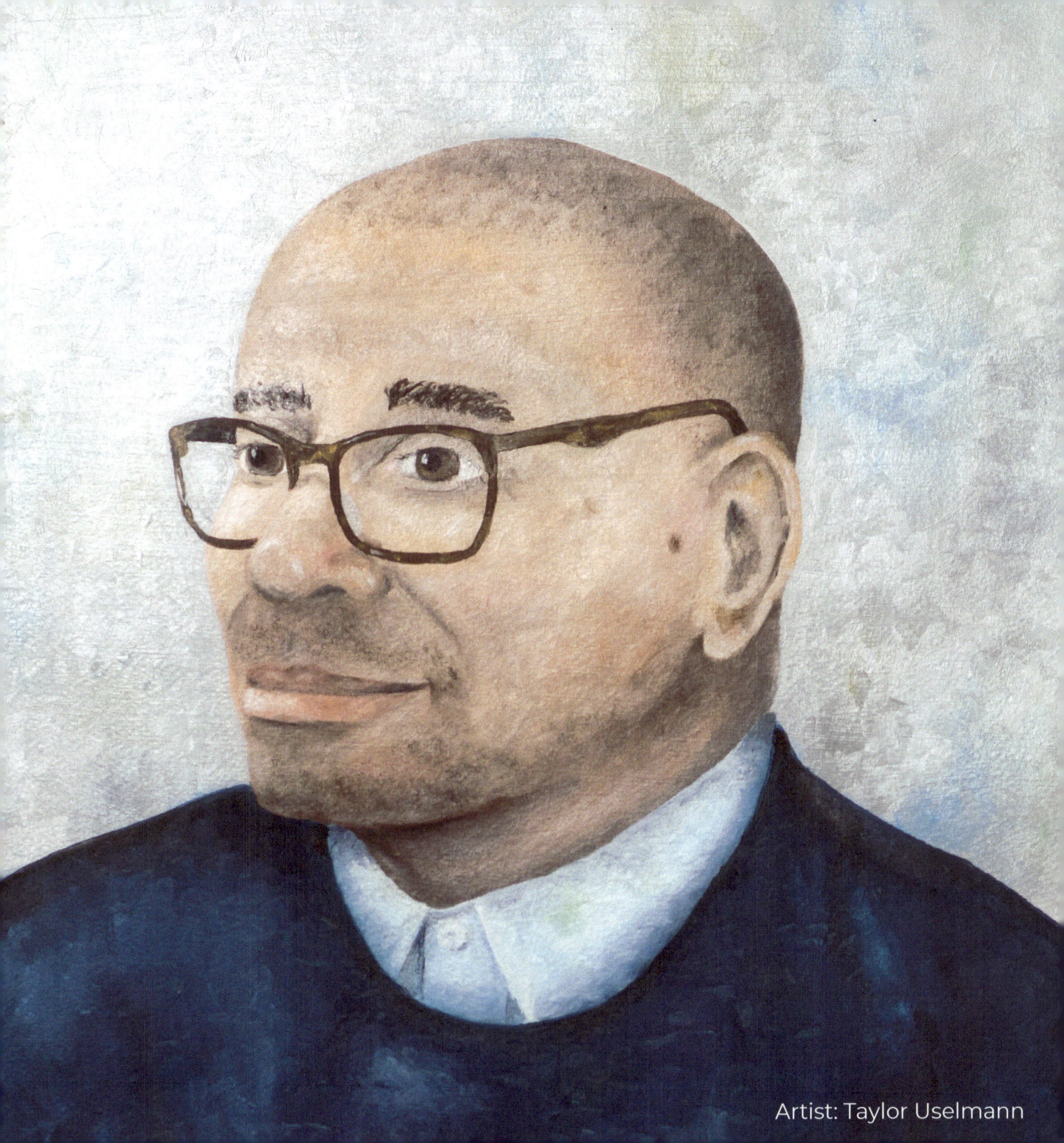

Artist: Taylor Uselmann

Jim Gannon

Showing up

Interview by Grace Egan, nominated by anonymous

I take a Cultural Studies class to Italy every year. We live in Florence and travel around; it's a travel writing course, and we travel around the northern and central parts of Italy... I don't know a lot of Italian, but the Italian language itself is incredibly beautiful. And I like the way that they view food... in a very kind of holistic way. It's something you can control; if you incorporate healthy food into your life, you become happier. Last summer, my students averaged almost 200 miles of walking over three weeks. You're just walking, you're moving, and you're eating well. You're drinking good wine... Being in Italy is a way of life. It's a way to approach things. I appreciate how much care they put into their food. [Italians] take food seriously, and I don't think we do here. There's an awareness... I think it's important to take food seriously, and I don't think we do here. Slowing down—eating—and appreciating it more would be important.

My grandfather was one of the hardest-working people I've ever known. Never missed a day of work. I can't say I've inherited his work ethic, but I've always admired it. And my mom. I was really close to my mom, and she also has an incredible work ethic; she's seventy-five years old [and] working as a crossing guard. Both of them are oddly optimistic even though they lived, not hard lives, but hard-working lives. They didn't have a lot of money at times, [but] they never got discouraged. They've both got really positive attitudes. And [my grandpa] was really tough; he never let challenges get him down.

My childhood was kind of... not pleasant. I had a somewhat violent stepfather, so my Grandpa taught me how to stand up for myself. How not to let things... dissuade me from what I wanted to do. He was resolute. Got up at 7:30. Ate at five o'clock. He taught me discipline, and how to survive. Growing up in Chicago, you have to be street smart. You have to take care of yourself.... He was probably the most fundamentally important person in my youth. He gave me hope... [And I learned] to be tough, in a mental way. Not like I was a bully, but tough [as in] don't let things stop you. In education, I see students who are able to overcome challenges, and students who get discouraged; not getting discouraged is the key, I think, to success. Sometimes you tell a student, "Ok. You have to revise this, this, and this," and they sit down and they do it. But other students are crushed by it, and they look the other way.

Yeah, my grandfather taught me the importance of showing up. And being disciplined. And not getting discouraged. There's more than one way to live an interesting life. You don't need a lot of money. You just need to be engaged with what you do.

The United States could learn a lot from Europe. That's what I hope. Europe does a lot of things right... Because there are more political parties, there's naturally more compromise... But the United States has always been a leader when it comes to big moral issues. And I think it still can. We have enough people and resources to do that. Europe can't and won't do that. The United States has to be a leader when it comes to international politics.

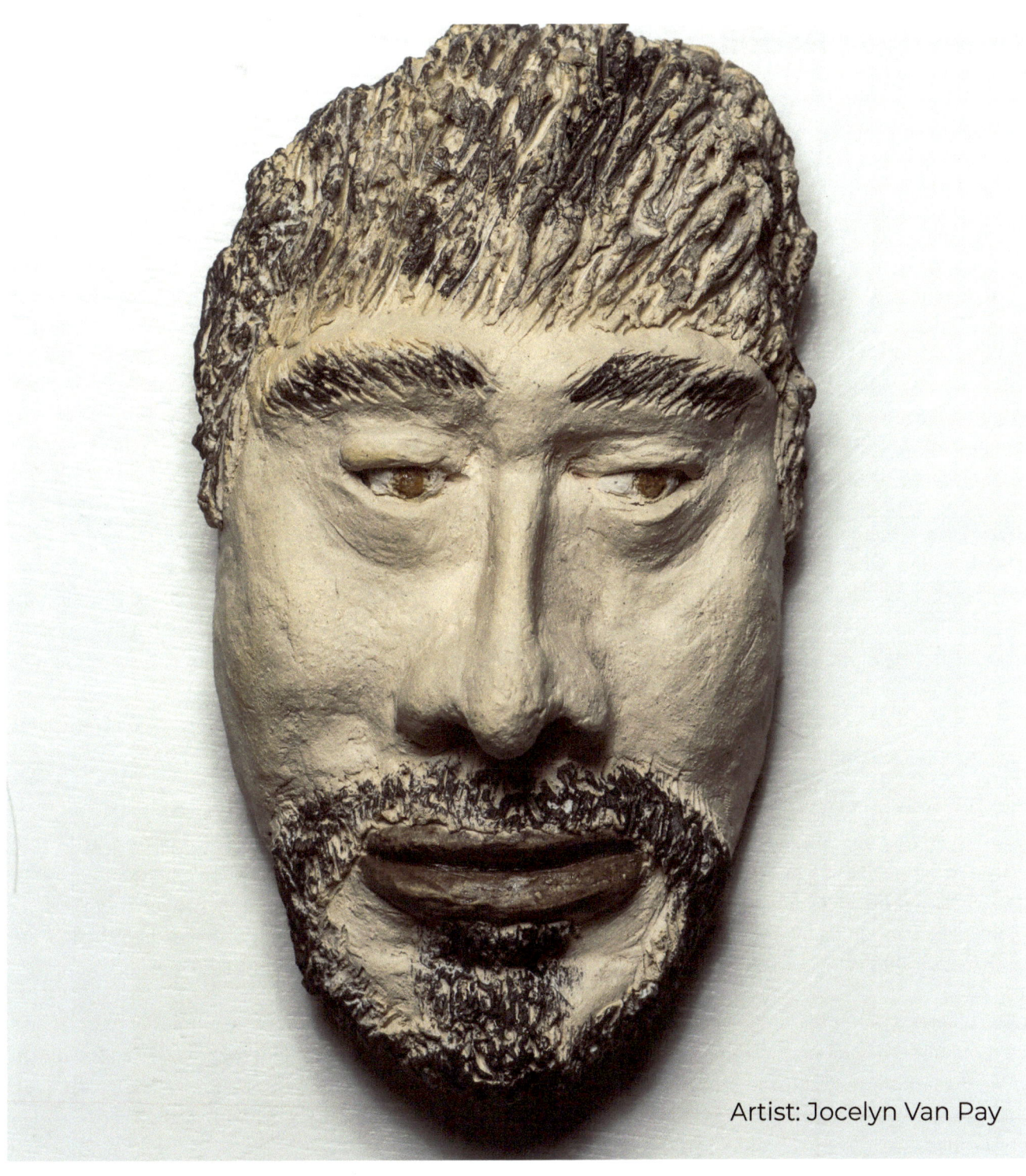

Artist: Jocelyn Van Pay

Kimberly A. Redding

Through the heart

Interviewed by Eleni Caprio, nominated by Greg Gabrielsen

When I was little, we always made our babysitters play school with us. I was always the teacher. Beyond that, I just read all the time. I was the kid who could lie on her bed all day with a book. I thought I was going to be maybe an editor, like an editor for a women's magazine—*Southern Living* or *Good Housekeeping*, something like that. Then, the first time I studied abroad, that was it. Since then, 10th grade, it's like I *have* to find ways to get back to Germany, back to Europe. I kind of fell in love with the culture… and also a few guys, one after the other. Personal relationships. And I came to study history through that, through my heart.

All through grad school, my advisor was actually pushing me to pursue the research track. But I would only apply for jobs that focused on teaching and student interaction, schools where that came first. He must have finally relented, because when Carroll was hiring, he knew somebody on Carroll's faculty. They ran into each other at some meeting, and my advisor said, "I have this advisee who is set and determined to be at a teaching school." That was good because I learned later that my application had been lost.

Looking back, there are two moments that really shaped my teaching career. I taught a class on my own in grad school, at UNC-Chapel Hill, the first class I'd taught by myself. And I'd been holed up someplace—my office or library cubby—totally oblivious that there had been an active shooter right on Franklin Street, shooting up over the hill toward the main lawn of the university. Nobody on campus was killed, but that's what the students brought into class because they had been outside and aware of it. I think what stuck with me about it is that as an instructor, I want students to *be* in class. That's the most important thing, right? "You're here now. Focus on my class. What do you mean, you didn't finish the homework?" But I try to balance that with knowing students have mental baggage. Who knows what they're carrying?

The positive moment was in the spring of 2010. My husband was ill and in a coma for about a month, and I was teaching and then going to see him. You never know, as a faculty member, how much of your personal life to share. Do you set it aside or do you bring yourself into the classroom? Do you tell students what's going on? And it's a small campus, so of course, people find out anyway. It's just, do you name the elephant in the room? I don't think I talked about it in *all* my classes, but in one class I did—it turned out a student's brother had died of the same cancer. And at the end of the semester, they gave me a gift card to take my kids to the movies.

It just creates a better learning environment when the students know that the professors are real people, and we remember that you are. We're on the same side, right? I mean, so often we kind of antagonize them, you know, the lazy students, the mean professors. But everybody on this campus is here, at least on their best days, because they want to learn stuff and they want to make the world a better place, in both a small sense and in a big sense.

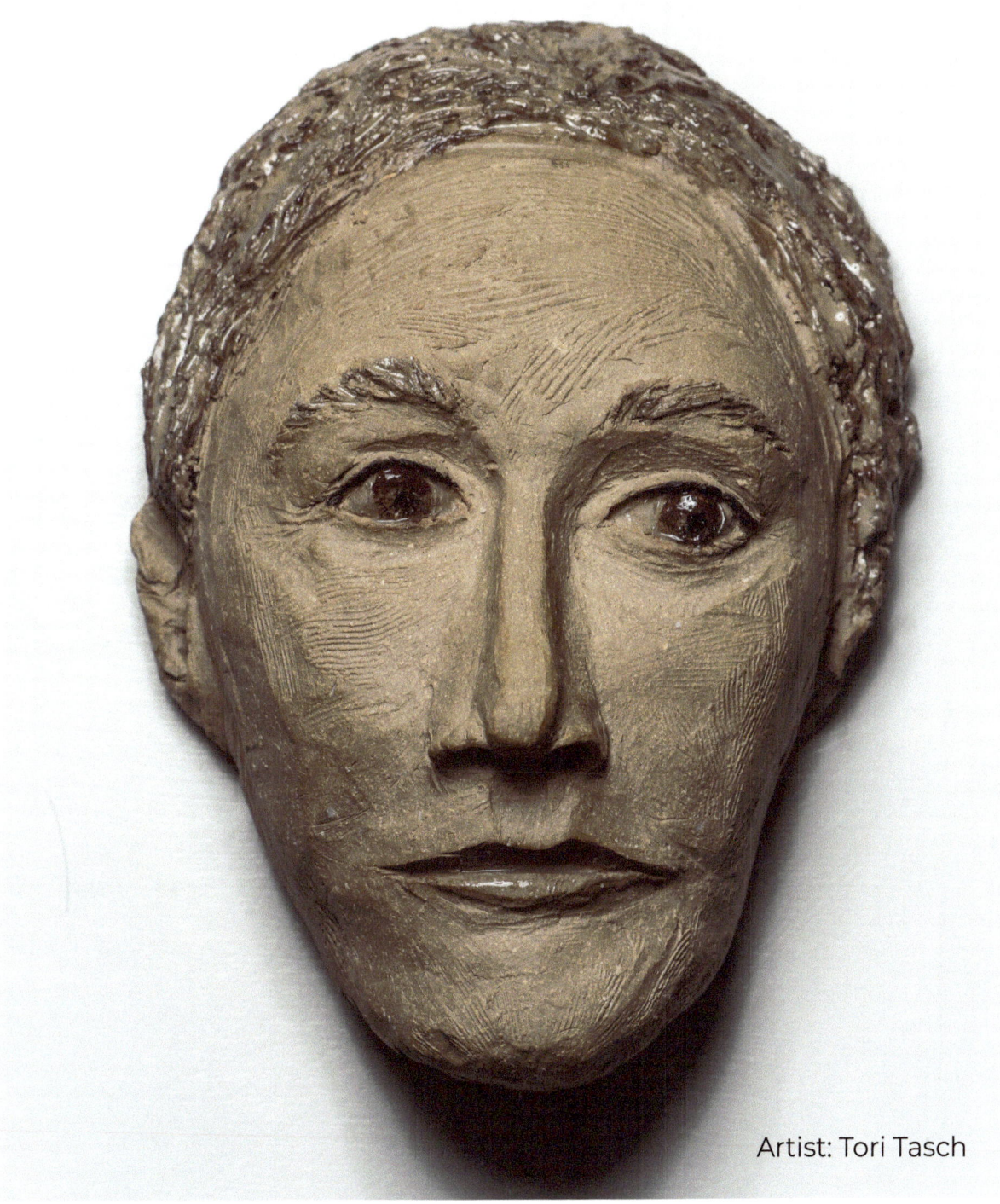

Artist: Tori Tasch

Sean Cunningham

Good at heart

Interviewed by Jessica Mattan and Ryan Rozanski, nominated anonymously

I was born in Florida, moved to Waukesha, and finally settled in Burlington, WI, where I've lived most of my life. I chose Carroll because it was one of the few schools in the area that offered a music therapy major with a benefit of being close to home. I chose music therapy because I love playing instruments and helping others. I play piano, also some violin and guitar. One of the best experiences I've had with music therapy was seeing my Grandma, who has impaired movement, dance and connect to one of her favorite songs. It was one of the happiest moments of my life.

I value the quality of life of others and always try to help those who are having a rough time with their lives. In high school, I used to work for the in-school suspension program at my high school. So there's detention; that's only 15 minutes or so at the beginning or end of the school day. Suspension is more serious. Those kids usually have stuff going on. They act out in school, break rules, but… there's something going on, even if you have no idea what it is. I met a student one time who seemed to be having a hard time. I don't know what was bothering him. It's like that for most of us, right? You don't know what's going on in someone's life. What they've done. What they've been through. Or what they're stuck in right now. I just said, "I hope everything goes well for you at some point," and he thanked me. Just for caring, or for saying that I cared. Even those kids in suspension are usually good at heart. Sure, they're in there, in suspension for some reason, a bad choice, or something they did. But there's more to it.

I believe everybody is put on earth for a reason. And music, or really thinking about creativity in general—if it's music, design, writing, whatever—any of it can tell a story. Some music just reaches into my soul. And there's always some story behind it. It's never the same. The music is maybe the same on the page, but when someone plays it, it becomes… it's just different. So yeah, I'm always thinking about how I can change the world for the better, leave my own legacy. I know, it's a big statement for a 19 year old.

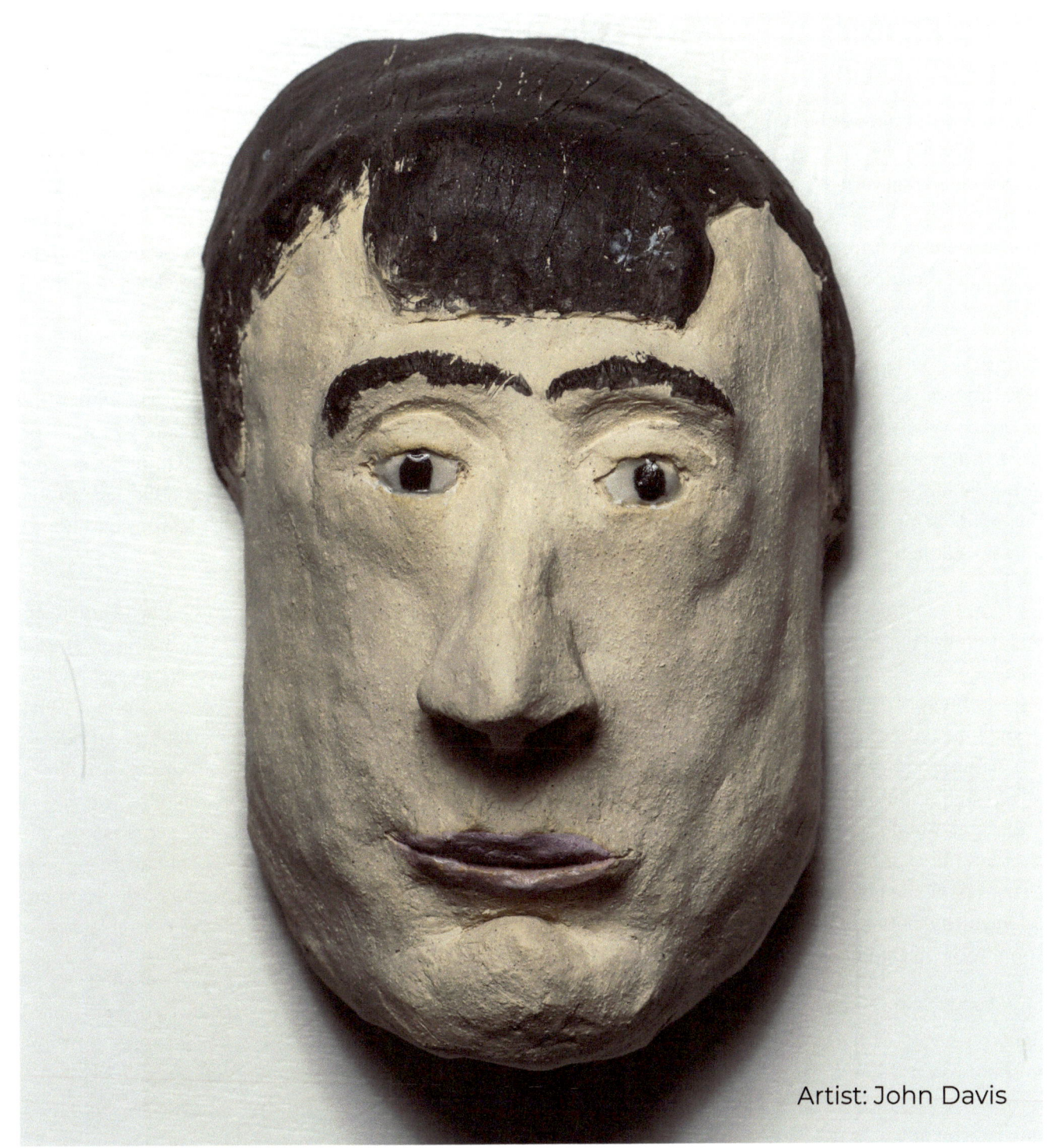

Artist: John Davis

Susie Foster
A little bit of faith

Interviewed by Megan Wagoner, Allison Winters, and Steven Grabowski, nominated anonymously

In coaching, you have the opportunity to have a direct impact on individual students over a longer period of time. You have the same group of students for four years, and we see them almost every day. So it's cool because you're really there for a lot of our students' big "aha" moments. Whereas as an administrator, you're kind of impacting change or influencing change... from an outside perspective. You're taking all those little lessons that you learned from direct interactions with students, and then you're saying, "OK, how can we work through policies and protocols to create an environment where our students, or our student athletes, can succeed?"

You need to experience all sorts of different things to gain that perspective. That's one of the most important things I learned growing up: not everybody thinks like you. Not everybody's raised in an environment like you like. Not everybody wants the same things out of life. And you know, that doesn't make one or the other right or wrong. What makes it interesting and special is to understand, to figure out, "Hey, here's where you stand or what you believe. But there's all sorts of other people in the world; how do you bring that all together?" ...It's about relationships... I think my parents were role models. And I was lucky to find a profession through sports that enables me to... have an avenue through soccer to be able to talk about all those life lessons and hopefully do a little bit of what I think my parents did for me growing up.

My biggest thing is... that when you have the chance to have a conversation with somebody, and you create an environment that's nonjudgmental and comfortable... it's amazing what you can learn. I think that's something really special about Carroll. It's not just about a small classroom, but it's also about the experience of having a go-to person, right? In Athletics, Student Success, the classroom, wherever, we try to have an impact. Most of the time, you probably never know if you do, but you hope that you have a fleeting impact on a student... [It's about] putting all of our students here in the driver's seat. How do we create an environment that allows any of our students to succeed, regardless of where they're going? Obviously, for us in Athletics, winning is important, but not just that, right? I mean, we want our students to come out with awesome degrees in whatever field they're choosing to study and to use some of those experiences on the athletic field as they go on to the rest of their life. I think my ultimate goal is, even if it's for a smidgen of time, can I have a positive impact on anybody that I come into contact with, regardless of if they're a soccer player? You know, even if I just see somebody on campus for five minutes, just trying to have that sort of positive impact.

I totally believe in the trickle-down effect. Influencing change on a large scale starts small-scale. And sometimes it's hard. You think, "Well... what...? Am I really making a difference? Who cares?" Because you don't get to see those actions come to fruition all the time... I mean, there's a billion people out there, right? Billions of people. So you have to have a little bit of faith in what [you're] doing and... hope that it makes an impact on one person at a time down the road.

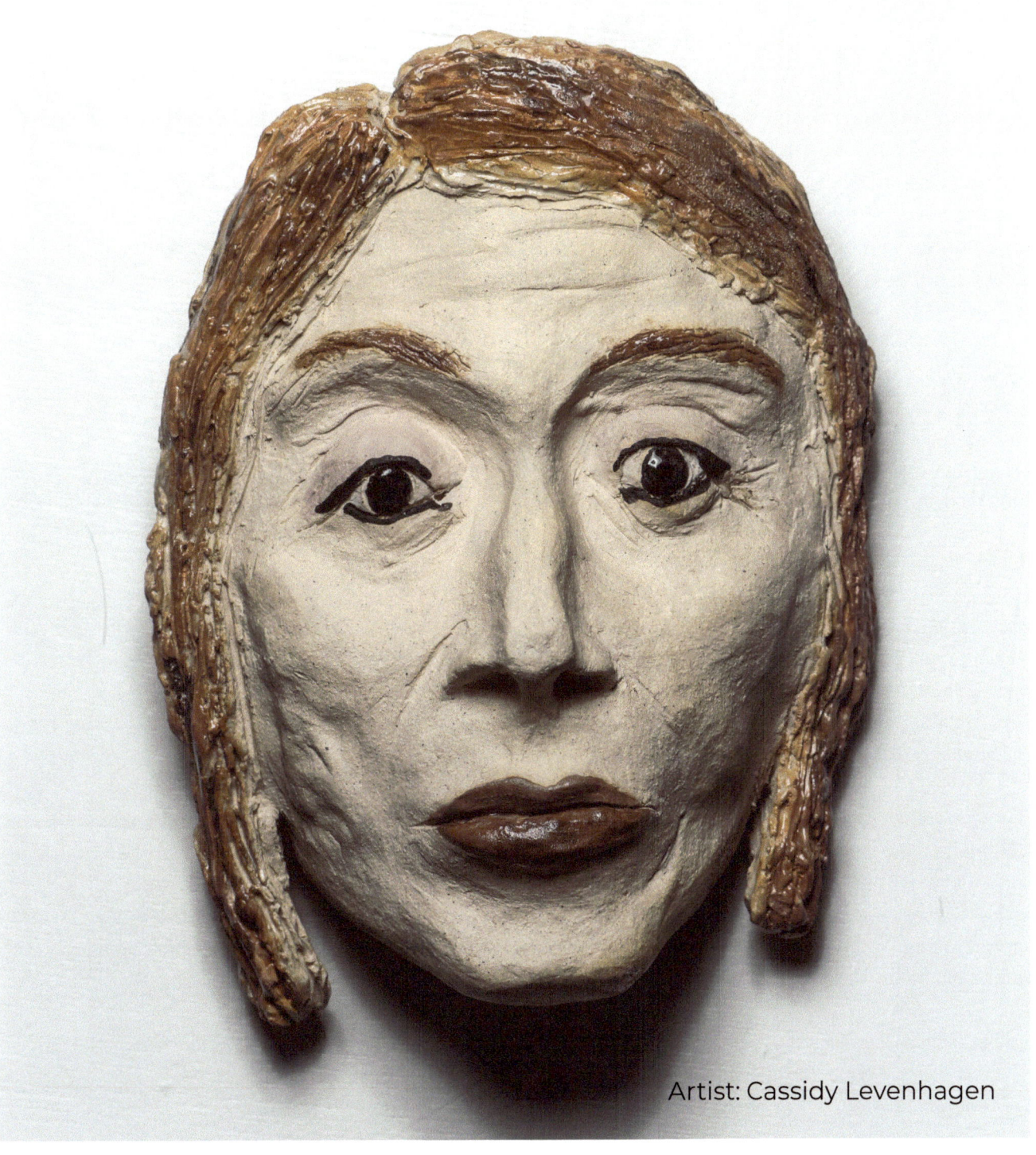

Artist: Cassidy Levenhagen

Dawn Scott
Bring me your student

Interviewed by Elaine Yarger, nominated by Elizabeth Brzeski

I grew up in the Upper Peninsula of Michigan, on the border with Wisconsin, in a very small town… My graduating class was 68 students. My parents have been divorced since I was four, so I had always had two sets of families: a stepmom and stepdad. And it was, it was sheltered. Growing up north, there's not a lot of things to do. You know, you have Wal-Mart, and that's it. So there weren't a lot of things to do, but it was nice—a lot of outdoor play, a lot of cousins, a lot of that type of thing… When it's small like that, there's a little bit of everybody's in everybody else's business, you know. I have a great family, but I sort of grew up on my own in a way because when I was 15, I moved out of my parents' home to move in with my grandma and grandpa… who lived in the town where the Wal-Mart is. I had to pay for a lot of my own things: books, supplies, and things like that. So I got a job so I could do extracurriculars in high school. And then I started saving for college.

I'm very passionate about telling people that I didn't grow up with money; I was a Pell Grant recipient. Especially with Carroll being a pricier school, I think that helps me understand that when a student comes here and they're paying hard-earned dollars—either theirs or their parents—how much they appreciate it. That's why I like to connect with my students a lot; I give the parents a hard time when I get to know them and not the student. I'm like "I want your student! Bring me your student; let me help them."

…I would never tell anybody to follow my footsteps in terms of a college career. I paid for college by myself, which meant I needed to work every minute I wasn't in class or studying. I had a few really solid friends. I didn't party, I didn't join orgs. I left my dorm room at 7am and I got back at 4:30pm. If I didn't have class at night, I studied; I needed good grades, needed to be able to pay for my own things. So that social part was very lacking. That was definitely the hardest part.

…I was an accounting major, and in my junior year I decided, "I love numbers, but if I can't work with people this accounting thing's not going to work for me." I eventually became part of the financial aid office. I was a student worker, and there were two ladies up front who sort of scooped me in, took me under their wing. It was just a perfect fit. The ladies I worked with were endearing and kind; they cared about our students. And that's who I wanted to emulate. That image of people having to be afraid of you to give you power is not something I ever want to emulate. I actually think you can do ten times more if you are friendly or caring about it.

I've certainly had struggles, but I don't look at them like that… My story is my story, and I live it, breathe it, love it. I know everybody has their own stuff. But I go back to positivity because I do think it will get you everywhere. Being negative about it isn't going to get you anywhere.

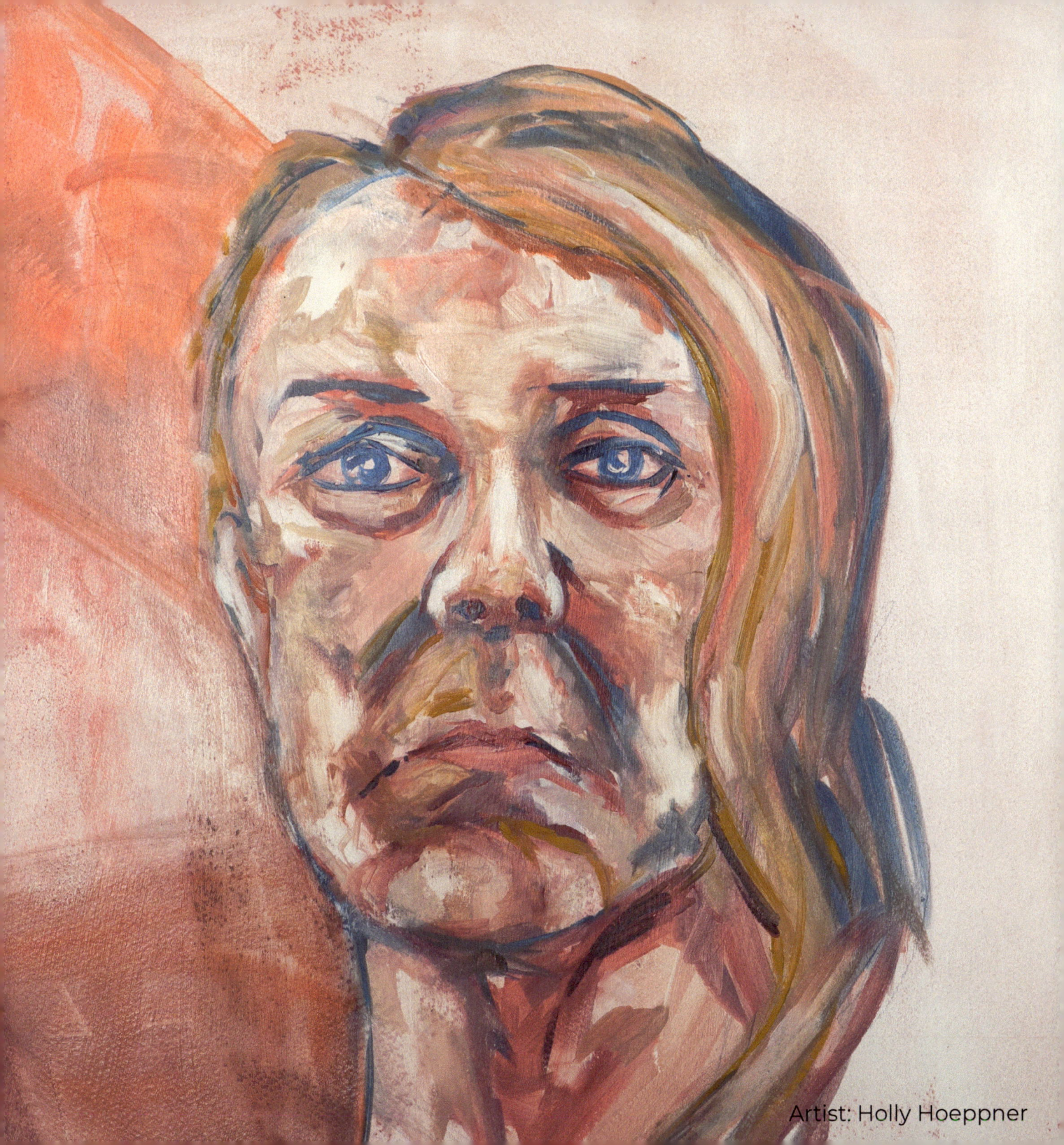

Artist: Holly Hoeppner

Mandy Balek-Stephens
You can always reevaluate

Interviewed by Natasha Pellegrini and Sadie DeGrand, nominated by Greg Gabrielsen

I always wanted to be a teacher—an educator, in some way—but I actually went to college at UW-Platteville planning to major in Marine Biology. After a few classes and some research, I switched to Phys Ed and Health Education. I taught in K-12 education for a bit and realized I wanted to work with college students. So I went back to school for Counselor Education and Student Services.

As an undergraduate, I'd been pretty active on campus. I was in a sorority, in student government… I was on the executive board of the college's Gay-Straight Alliance, but I wasn't ready to come out as a gay woman yet. I was actually forced to come out by a sorority sister, and then I decided to tell my family. It was rough [until] I finally found my soulmate, Jenna. We have joint custody of my son, Roman. He was at our wedding, [and] I'm finally happy, living life, and being the person I want to be. I still struggle with this sometimes, but if I can't love myself or be myself, how can I expect anyone else to love or be themselves?

I strive to learn from others, even when I'm teaching or supervising them. In those kinds of positions, [you have to] stand up for what you believe in, but also listen. Every time I meet someone new, I want to learn as much from them as they learn from me. I value other people a lot, and that has led to some great people in my life. I'm always looking for something new to do or try to accomplish, and a lot of that curiosity and drive comes from talking with other people, whether it's new students trying to find a major or changing directions for some reason… or faculty and staff from different parts of campus.

Anyone who has that passion for exploring, for learning, I want to talk with them. That's how I grow, and that's how I've gotten into different professional positions. I was working as an Academic Advisor at UW-Parkside when I first saw the job opening for Assistant Director of Advising here at Carroll. I was working with something like 350 advisees at Parkside, but I didn't think I was qualified enough for the position of Assistant Director. After three different colleagues (all of them outside Wisconsin!) sent me the job posting, I decided to take a leap of faith and apply. Is that a strategy? I don't know. It works for me.

I have gained more responsibility since coming to Carroll, and that's what I was looking for. I see myself here for a long time, even though I drive over two hours a day; I would like that to change in the future. But you can always reevaluate. As Roman gets older, we can see what we want to do at that point. It can change. All I really want is to enjoy my job and be able to spend time with the people I love.

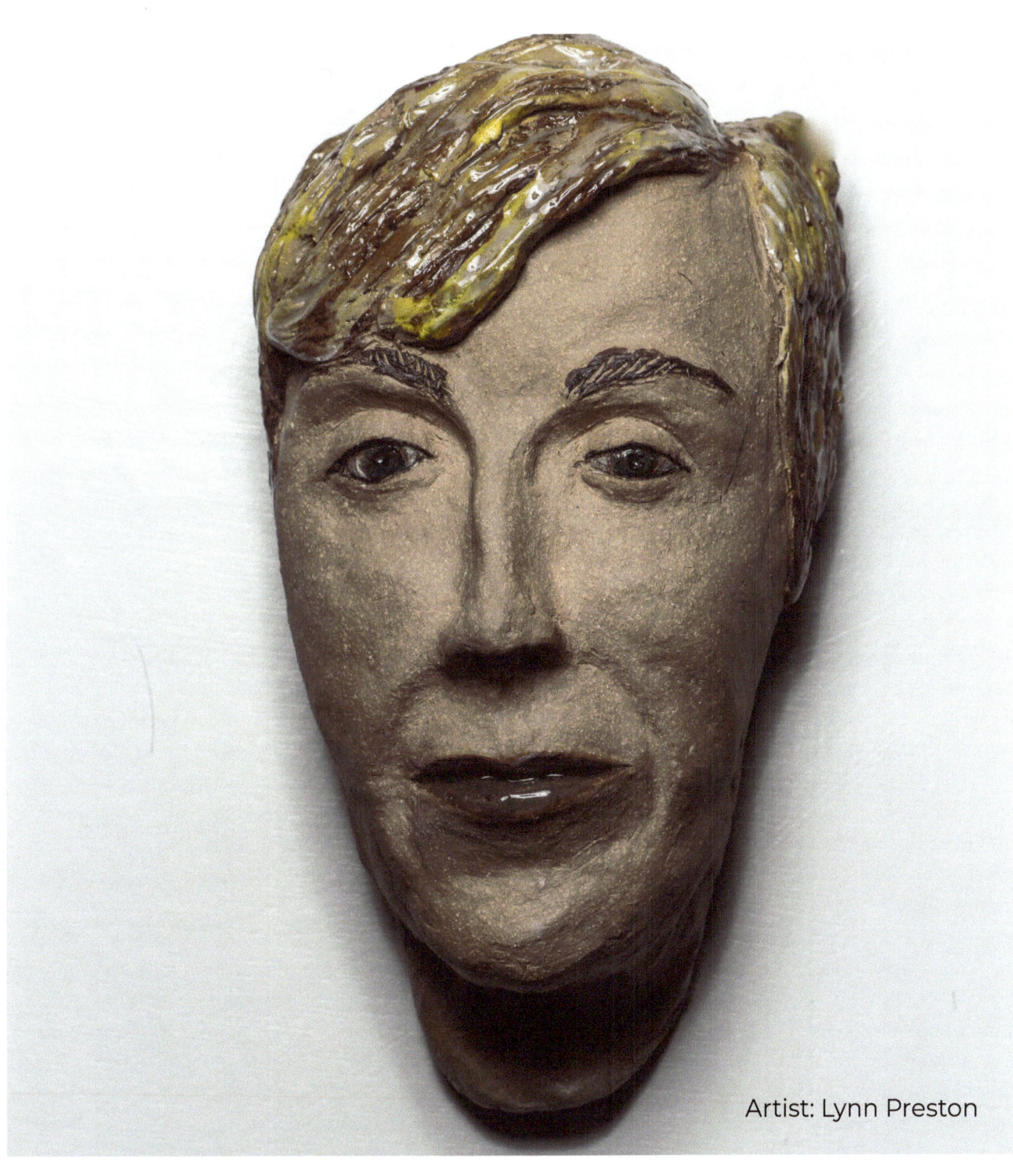

Artist: Lynn Preston

Jamie Hansen

Never say never Interviewed by Michael Jankovic and Kate Gentry, nominated by anonymous

My motivation is the students. I mean, first and foremost, I'm here because I want to have good nurses out in the workforce. I want people to be passionate about nursing just like I am. That's something that drives me to do a good job. I don't want to just show up to class and not be prepared, or not be excited about the topics that I'm talking about. In Medical Surgical Nursing, the students are excited; they want to learn about that. But Nursing Research, not so much. So I have to find ways to make it relatable to them, to what they're doing right now. I try to get them to understand, "Why is this important for you? Why do you need to understand this?" And yes, this is, this can even be exciting; even nursing research can be exciting. I try to bring that into the classroom.

I had a professor at WCTC who was down to earth and very understanding. You could let your guard down a little bit, show your personality and not always be super serious like sometimes people are. That professor never said anything that would make you feel bad about yourself as a student. So I really try to think about those sorts of things when I'm talking with students because I know that a lot of them are going to have struggles, a lot of them are going to have some setbacks, but does that mean that they're not going to be a great nurse? Absolutely not. And so I don't… I try to think about myself and what I went through, struggles I might have had during nursing school and then [respond] like that professor. It's ok; you don't need to be so serious all the time.

When I went to school for my associate's degree, I said, "OK, I'm going to go for my bachelor's degree, and that'll be it. I'll be done. Then, after I had my kids and I was thinking about going back to school, I'm like "OK, I'll get my master's degree, then I'll be done… I would never want to do research… I don't want to do that." Then there was talk about going back for a PhD and how important research would be for that. I thought, "Oh gosh, I don't really want to do this." But I had somebody–another faculty member who had worked here previously–who encouraged me: "You'll be fine. You can do it." I was thinking, "Really? I don't think I can," but then I went back for my PhD at Marquette and got into research. I really like it now, and [learned] that I shouldn't tell myself, "No, no, no, I'm not interested in that ever, ever, ever," because it seems like the path ends up going whatever way it's supposed to go anyway.

The faculty we work with are all… They share that passion about nursing, and they're here for the students… Some students might need a little bit more guidance than others, but it's just a different process for everybody. Some people come in and they don't know much about nursing. [Others] had family members who are nurses; they've been surrounded by it their whole lives. It's a little bit different for everybody. I don' t really see myself leaving education… I don't want to say I'll *never* do anything different because, well, I've learned that part. But I do want to continue my research, and I really like teaching. So we'll see what happens.

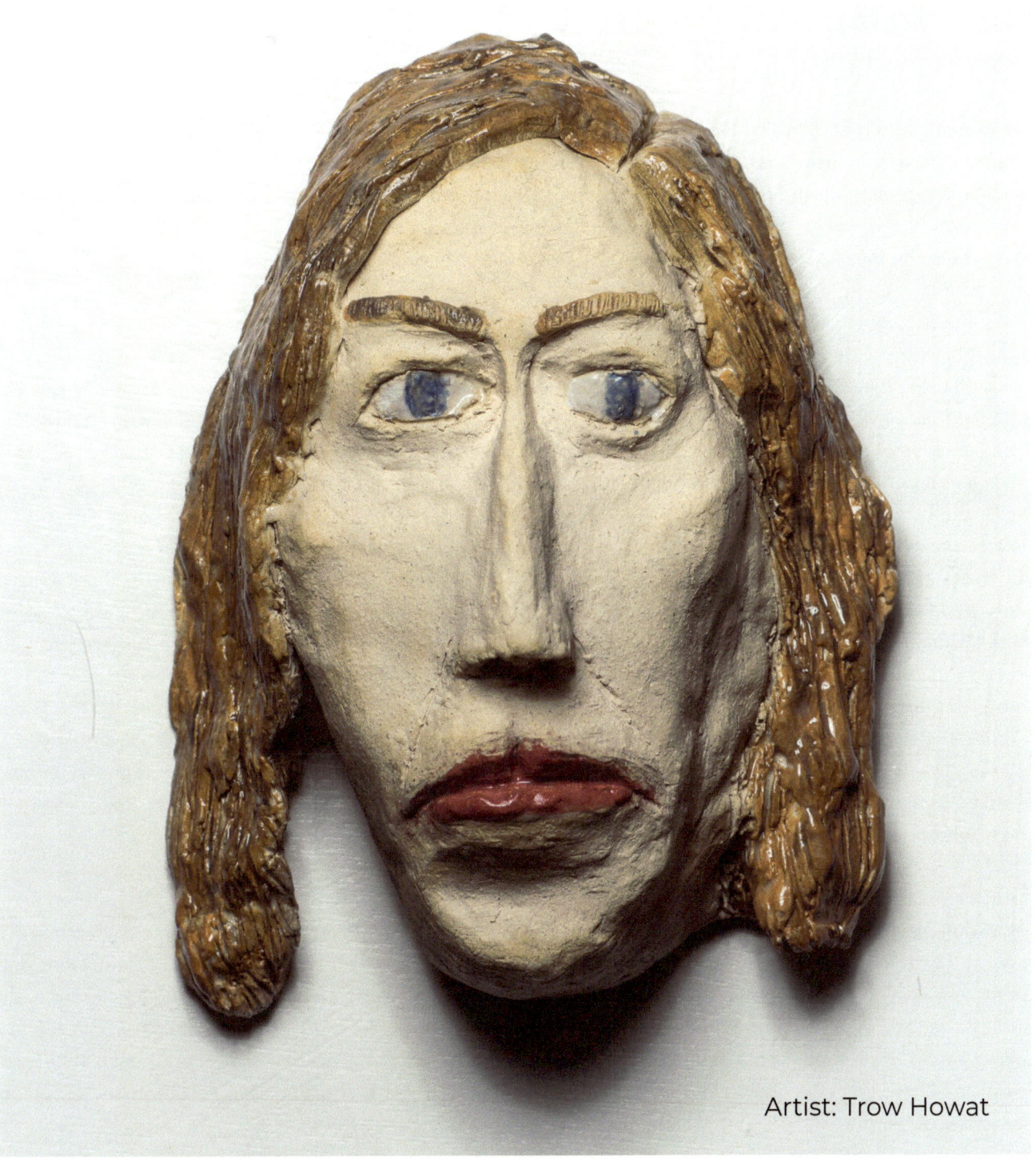

Artist: Trow Howat

Mark Wampfler

Doing a good job

Interviewed by Katie Sweeney and Saskia de Rooy, nominated by Sara Meyer

Ever since starting at Carroll, I kind of had it in my mind that I wanted to be a teacher because my favorite teachers instilled in me a passion for what they do: my band teacher, obviously, but I also had a great English teacher in high school who really changed my mind about reading and writing. That was something I had kind of struggled with, but he was such a great teacher; he gave me a passion for reading and writing… I wanted to do the same thing.

I had thought about being a composer, a performer, or a soloist. I was sure that if I went into teaching, I would get a job, whereas performer and composer are more... risky. You have to be really, really, really good to make a living off those things. I knew that if I became a teacher, I could still perform. I could train to be as good a teacher as I could possibly be but then also perform and compose while teaching. Looking back on it now, I realize that being as good of a teacher as I possibly could set me up to be as good of a learner as I could so that I could learn more about performing and composing and have the best of all of those different worlds.

I started teaching in the middle of coronavirus, so it's been a wild year. I teach sixth graders, and we have a separate section called Beginning Band for them; they're just starting instruments. The reason is because in sixth grade, they're required to take a music class, either band, choir, orchestra, or a world music class. So some of them join band thinking that they will really enjoy it, but some join just because they're required to take something. And of course, some kids find that they don't enjoy it. That's normal; they're experimenting to find things that they like, and not everybody can like band. There's one student in particular who said, "You know, I joined the band because I had to, and I didn't think I would like it… but I'm totally joining band next year. I love it! I love playing clarinet. My family loves when I play the clarinet." She's all in, full speed ahead, joining band next year. That's why I became a teacher! Not everybody can enjoy music as much as I do. But if I can help those who do enjoy it, I'm doing a good job. That was a really inspiring moment.

It can be really difficult for students who are just learning to play an instrument because they get wrapped up in "How do I play that note?" or "What's that note? How does that go?" And they forget to listen to each other. But now, at this point in the year, I'm seeing more students get excited… We just played their first duet. Up to this point, they've all played the same thing all together. And then they learned a piece that has two different parts, and they're like, "Wow, that's really cool!" Whether it be performing or helping teach people music or even just taking a weird instrument home and letting my family try it out... anything like that, that gives them a little bit of joy is, you know, that's everything for me. If I'm not teaching music, I'm doing something else with music… I feel like what I do–and what I'm doing with my students–is going to be there forever.

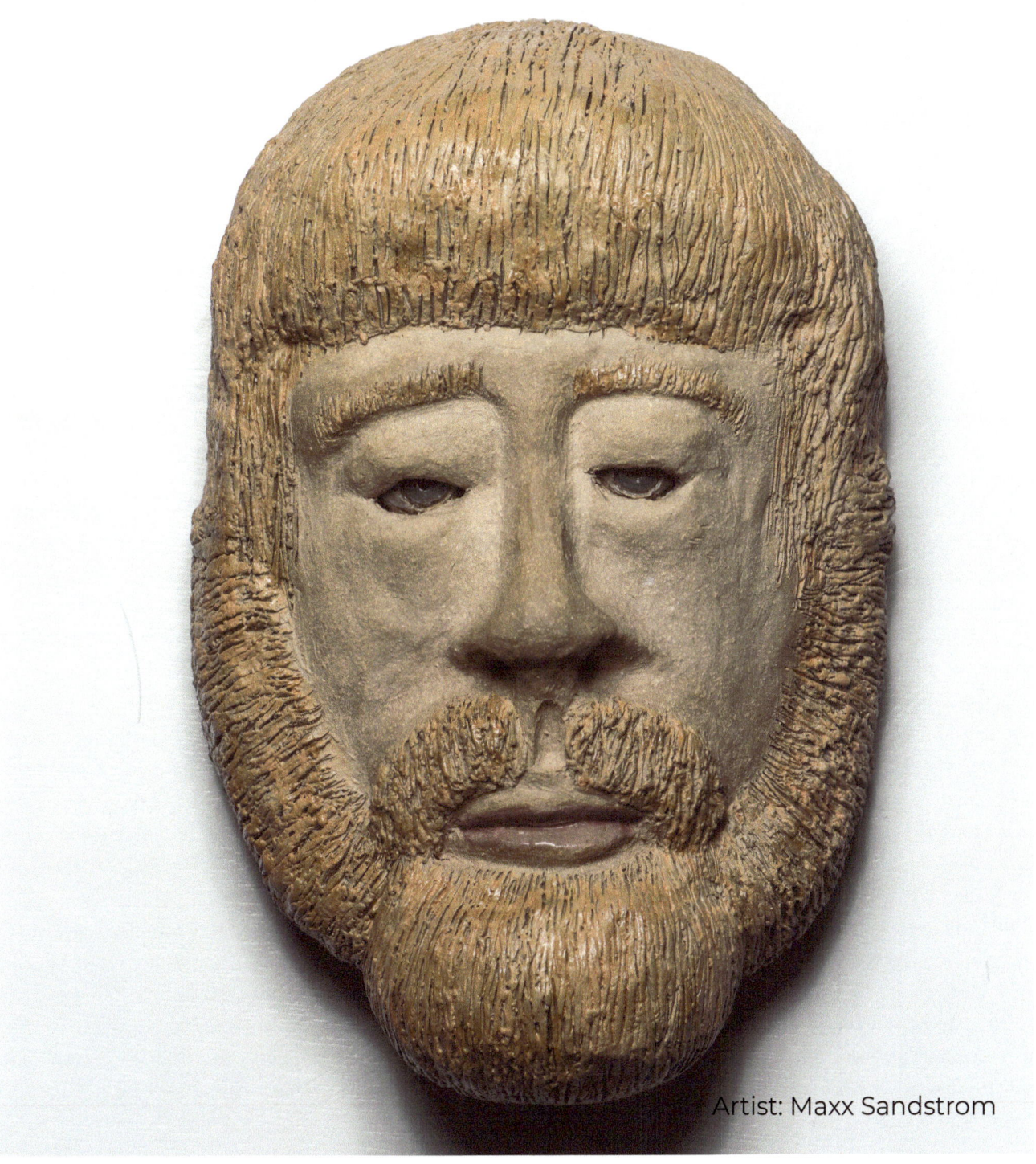

Artist: Maxx Sandstrom

Gerard DePons
A thing that's rare

Interviewed by Peter Loose, nominated anonymously

I worked at Pabst Brewery. That's how I started working… the first ten years. It was an old brewery, and they had underground caverns that were half buried. There was one that you could sneak down into. It was kind of cool. [Working there] helped shape me into who I am today. Then I was in construction. I was a carpenter for twenty, thirty years. I worked down at Abbot Laboratories at least three times. We would remodel all the labs… I had an accident building my own garage and I could no longer do construction. So I had to find something I could do, so I started here [at Carroll]. Actually, I started here in custodial, believe it or not. They were looking for maintenance people, and I always had a construction background, and that's why I got in maintenance.

I enjoy the kids at Carroll because I think it's nice seeing young people doing well… I have three kids and they're all in college or were all in college. One just graduated from here, and she's going to Marquette now. Marquette has a program where you can be in a health science major or whatever, and then they'll train you to be a nurse, and you get a master's that way. My second daughter goes to La Crosse. She's trying to get into… first she wanted to be a counselor. And now she's thinking she does very well at getting people grants and stuff. So she's trying to get into where she can help people get money for college, get set up for college. Because it does help the people that are going to college. They don't know, I don't know, what the government is offering this year versus last year.

When people are younger, they don't need to be chastised. They need to be nurtured or safe. When you make a mistake, or you're not sure about something, they say ,"Hey," like a good teacher. "You can do it." Actually, my mother was a teacher. Back then, it was a two-year degree, which would have been in the 40s. [She] went to college in Oshkosh, and she taught for about three months. The reason she said she quit was because she didn't like kids. But then she went and had twelve kids! Back then, the father just kind of worked. You know what I mean? The mothers were more stay-at-home, and everybody in my neighborhood had at least five kids. It was different… because back then everybody had larger families. Now you can't afford it. Today it's rare…

I'll tell you another thing that's rare. It's really great for your mom to have had a vision of what she could accept and what she could do…A lot of times, people think they could stay at home, and then they start staying at home to take care of kids. And they realize they can't do it. You know why? Because it's a routine. I got the laundry, and I'm always here… it's like cabin fever, you know what I mean? There's a lot of people that, they can't do that today… There's always media being thrown at you: "Hey, look what you could do! Why don't you ever try *this*, or why don't you…" Not a lot of people anymore know what they can accept, and do it.

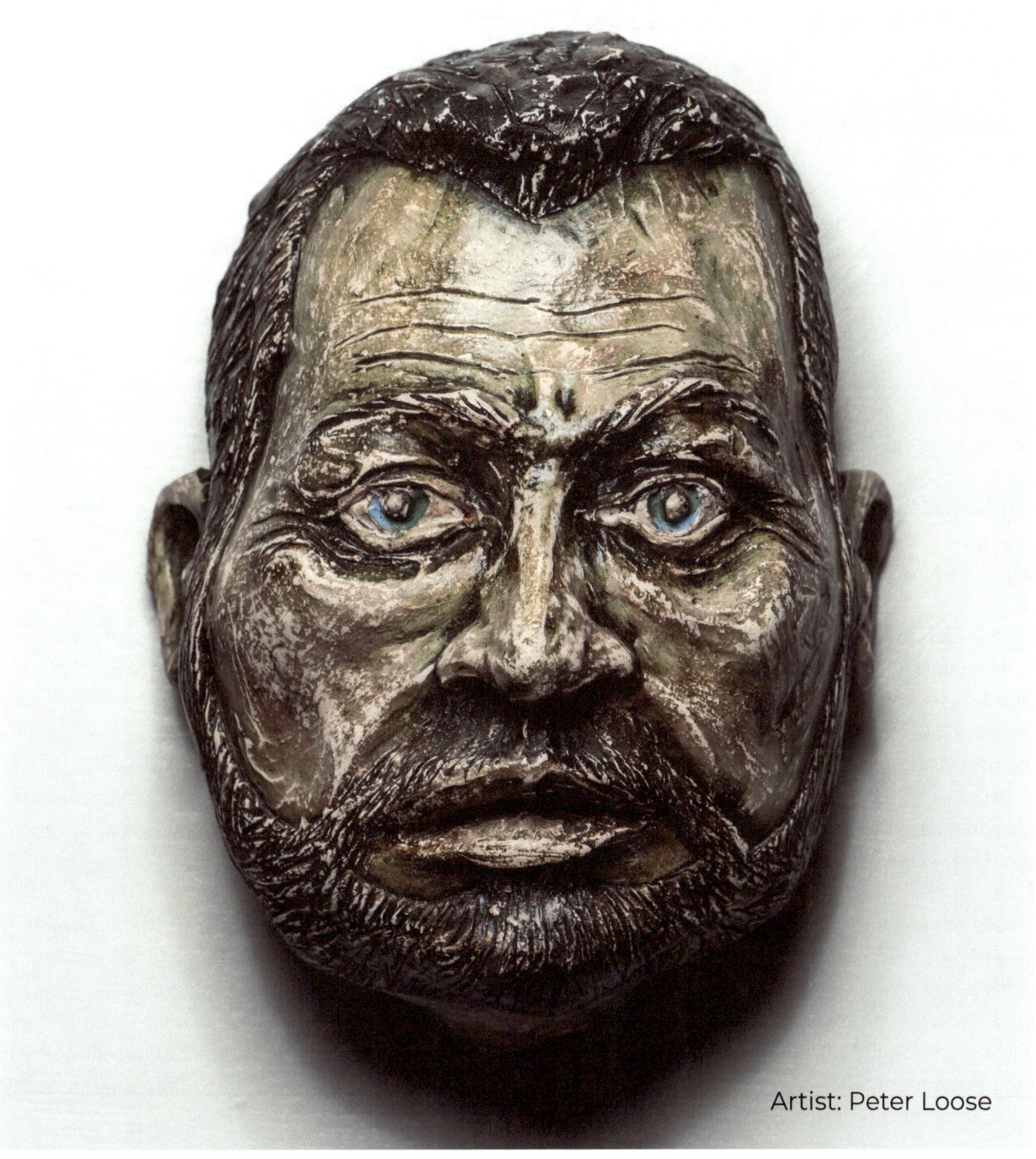

Artist: Peter Loose

Jessica Perez

Everything happens for a reason　　　*Interviewed by Elaine Yarger, nominated by Kaitlyn Cornella-Carlson*

Right now, I'm working full-time and going to school part-time, so I'm super busy. I'm majoring in psychology with a minor in sociology. I actually applied to Carroll right out of high school, but it was very expensive. So I was looking at other options, and I went to WCTC for medical language interpreting, and I did that. I got my certificate, and then I was like, "Oh, I think I want to do something else. Well, my mom works here [in dining services], and so she's like, "Hey, you should come and work here, and then you can get free credits every semester." So I did that. I worked for a year, then I started school again. I started with marine biology, [and then] switched over to psychology, and I love it.

I'm passionate about just helping people in general. I think I'm a big helper, even if someone's rude to me… I feel like it's just in me to try and help people… We all pre-judge people, but sometimes, I feel like a certain person might not be so nice; I can go on and on about that person. But then you get to know them, and you think, "Maybe I shouldn't judge people like that." When I was younger, there was this kid who said he was in a certain group… Once we were in high school and getting to know each other, he said "Hey, I'm so sorry that I ever picked on you when we were little because you're such a cool person." I was like, "Wow." It takes a lot to say something like that. I really appreciated that.

My happiest moments would be when I'm with my family because we're kind of separated. A lot of my mom's family is in Mexico. Most of my dad's family is here, but I just I love it when we're all together. My mom is from Guadalajara and my dad from Monterrey, which is a little more north. My mom is from the big city, and my dad is from the ranch. When we go to Mexico every summer, those would be my happiest moments… I've learned to appreciate them more because I'm not always there. I've had family members pass away once when I'm not there or when I'm [not] able to go afterwards. There was a year when a lot of people were passing away. My grandma passed away; my grandpa passed away. And then, all of a sudden, one of my uncles passed away, too. That was definitely the saddest moment, that streak…I just appreciate them.

I really want to work with trauma: PTSD in the military and police officers and stuff like that. So that would be very ideal. I don't know what else I really like at this point… I for sure still want to have my family with me, if that's possible. And everything else I guess is whatever happens. [I worry] that I won't find something in my field; one of my professors said that we possibly couldn't find anything without a master's degree. I don't know if I want to do that, so I'm really hoping that I can find something… just looking into the future with positive thoughts and hopefully things will just fall together. I couldn't think of one [thing I'd do differently]. If I really think about it, my motto is everything happens for a reason.

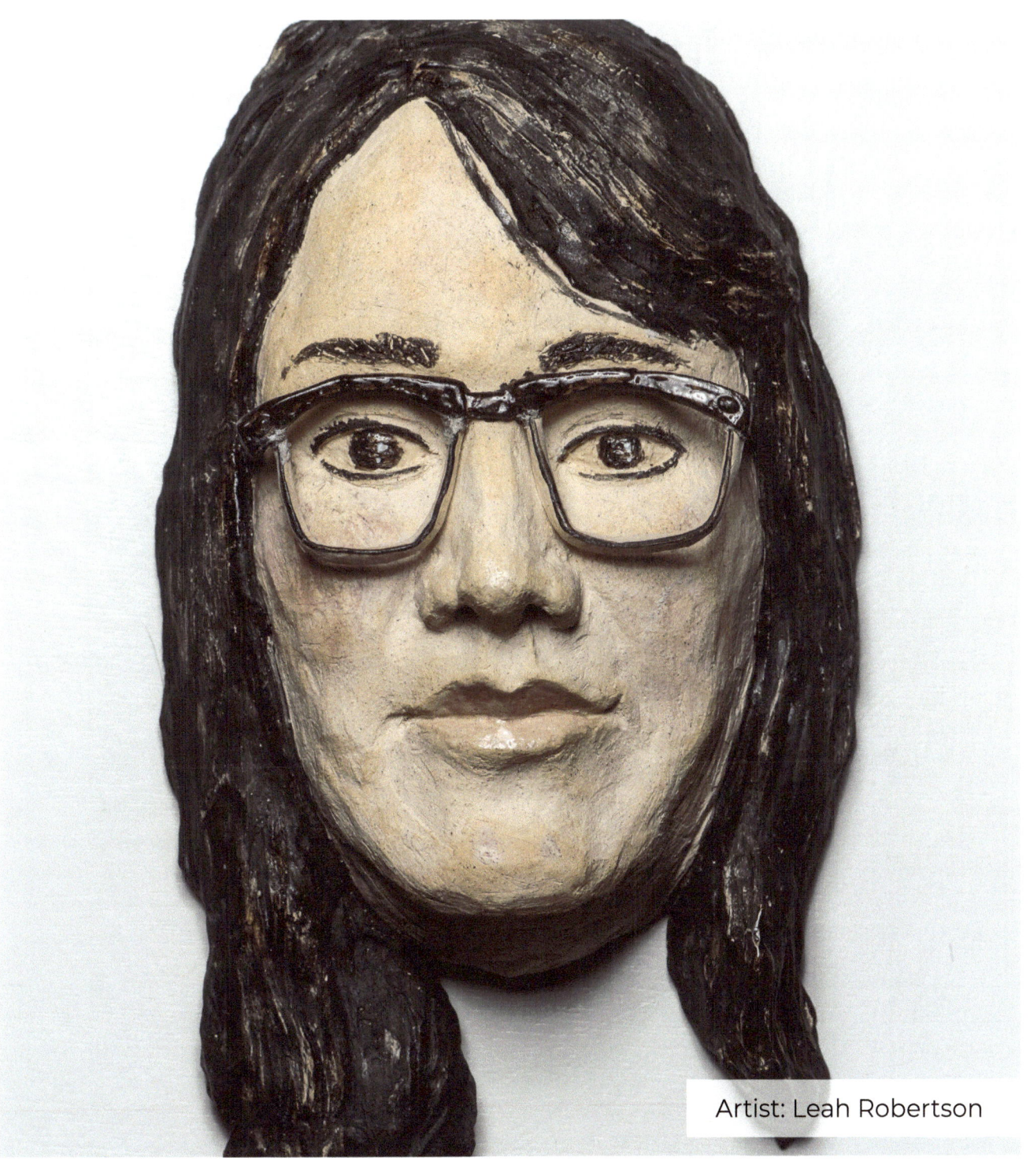

Artist: Leah Robertson

Shelby Stephan

Open mind, open heart

Interviewed by Julia Nelson, nominated anonymously

I'm a nursing student; the nursing program brought me to Carroll because it's really good, and I liked that it was a small school. That's very nice. I don't like big schools, and it gives you the option to get one-on-one with teachers and get more information. You get a lot more out of it… I continue to stay here because of my friends. Before I came here, school was a big factor in my life, but I didn't really care as much. When I came here, I totally did a 180°. That was with the help of them. It's not like we compete on grades, but them doing well almost makes me want to do better and study harder.

It encourages you to do better, and almost gives you the motivation to actually not be lazy and get up out of bed and stuff. One of my roommates, she's not a nursing major at all, but she… I'm thankful for her because she puts up with us just talking about it all the time. That also helps me, shapes me, and makes me realize I can't talk about this all the time. Other people have other stuff going on. It helped me not worry about myself so much. Coming here, they made more… it's an open mind, open heart type thing.

"Treat people how you want to be treated" is what I try to live by because you never know what the person next to you is going through. Sometimes even a simple "Hi," just smiling at someone in the street might help them feel more empowered, feel better about themselves. That's probably the biggest lesson my mom taught me: treat people how you want to be treated. It just… makes sense.

I think I wanted to be in the nursing program because my grandparents were both in and out of the hospital, especially my grandpa when I was younger. I was always there, and when he was in the ICU, I remember the gowns and the gloves that [the staff] literally stuffed in my bag for play–to play house and stuff. They made me comfortable with the situation and made me want to help others like they helped my grandparents.

Nursing is one of the things I think I could learn to really be passionate about. At first, I was a little iffy, but now I'm in clinicals and more involved. It's completely eye-opening: you see all these people who just need help, and it's kind of cool just giving them that help and being there for them, just talking to them–it makes them feel like a person. I like how you feel good because you did something that day besides just nursing. I feel like that almost motivates them to feel better, to get healthier, to get where they want to be.

One of the big things in nursing goes back to the fact that you don't know what people are going through. When people come in, for example, they look like they have diabetes and haven't done anything to treat it. There could be underlying things: maybe they can't afford their medications. You really have to be very open-eyed and have no biases because when someone comes in looking like they haven't been taking care of themselves, they're not just noncompliant. Most of the time, there's something going on in their life. There's always something else going on; as a nurse you have to talk to them and figure it out so you can help them through that.

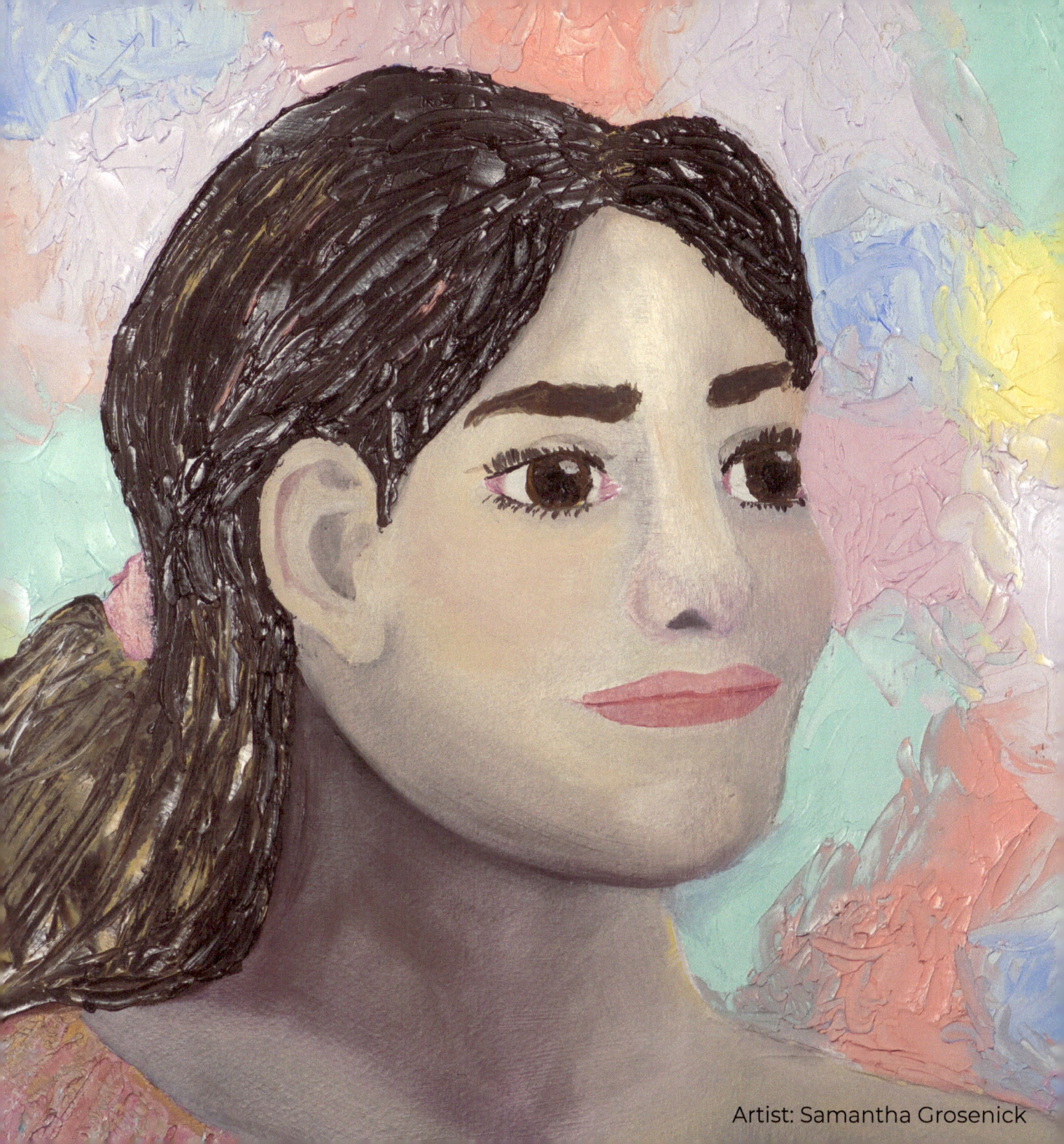

Artist: Samantha Grosenick

Anjana Adhikari
So much to learn

Interviewed by Saskia de Rooy, nominated anonymously

We are not a typical Nepali family. In a typical family, the son always gets priority. He doesn't have to do any chores. He gets a better education. He gets to go to private schools. He gets more pocket money, and he doesn't have any responsibilities at home while he is studying. The girl is supposed to… do her studies. Be home on time. Help with household chores and also bring a bit of dignity to the family. [But in my family], I was always sent to private school… I lived with my aunt just so I could go to a better private school. I was told to be independent and make my own decisions. My parents trusted me.

Carroll was a happy accident. I had taken a gap year gap [because] I wanted to do something in society and figure out who I am. My best friends started medical school and nursing school. So I had this pressure from home: "You're serving society, you haven't joined the university yet. Whereas your friends, they know what they're going to do in their life… And you don't. Where do you see yourself after six or seven years?"

I saw that I could do something for the children in Nepal while I was still just a high school graduate. So I started an organization… It was going fine, [but] I wasn't fully knowledgeable. I had a heart to help, but I didn't have the knowledge to serve them. I wanted the children to look back at me as a knowledgeable woman, not only a person with a good heart. So I went to a Nepali university, [but] it was full of politics, with political riots every day. Classes used to be disturbed by political leaders and groups coming in. I was frustrated with the education system and I needed an escape… So I went to a United States Education Fund office in Kathmandu… and found Carroll—it was the only place I applied.

I came here as a biology student to do genetic engineering. Freshman year, we had a general chemistry class. I'd learned the same topics in high school, but we never went into depth; it was always surface level. Here, I was like, "I don't know this. I didn't know that. I didn't know that would… There's so much to learn! Everything is chemistry!" I'm going into a research field. If you are a chemistry undergrad back home, you have to be a teacher or a professor. But there's so many pioneering things that you can do: You can start a research lab [or] a quality control lab, which Nepal still doesn't have. We have medicinal herbs in the mountains… We could extract chemicals and toxins from them and export them. I saw that I could go back home and do something, pioneer something…

I tell [friends] what I'm going to earn at my research job. They're like, "Only that much?" …I'm doing what I want to do. I'm going into the field I'm interested in. I'm more than happy with how much I will earn from this job rather than how much I get, you know? I remember how much I can do back home… People don't understand that living a life means, well, it's not all about money. They're so focused on buying extravagant stuff and living in a home with a pool and everything, and they don't see anything beyond that. That's the problem Nepal has right now; that's the problem this country has, too, [and] every other country in the world.

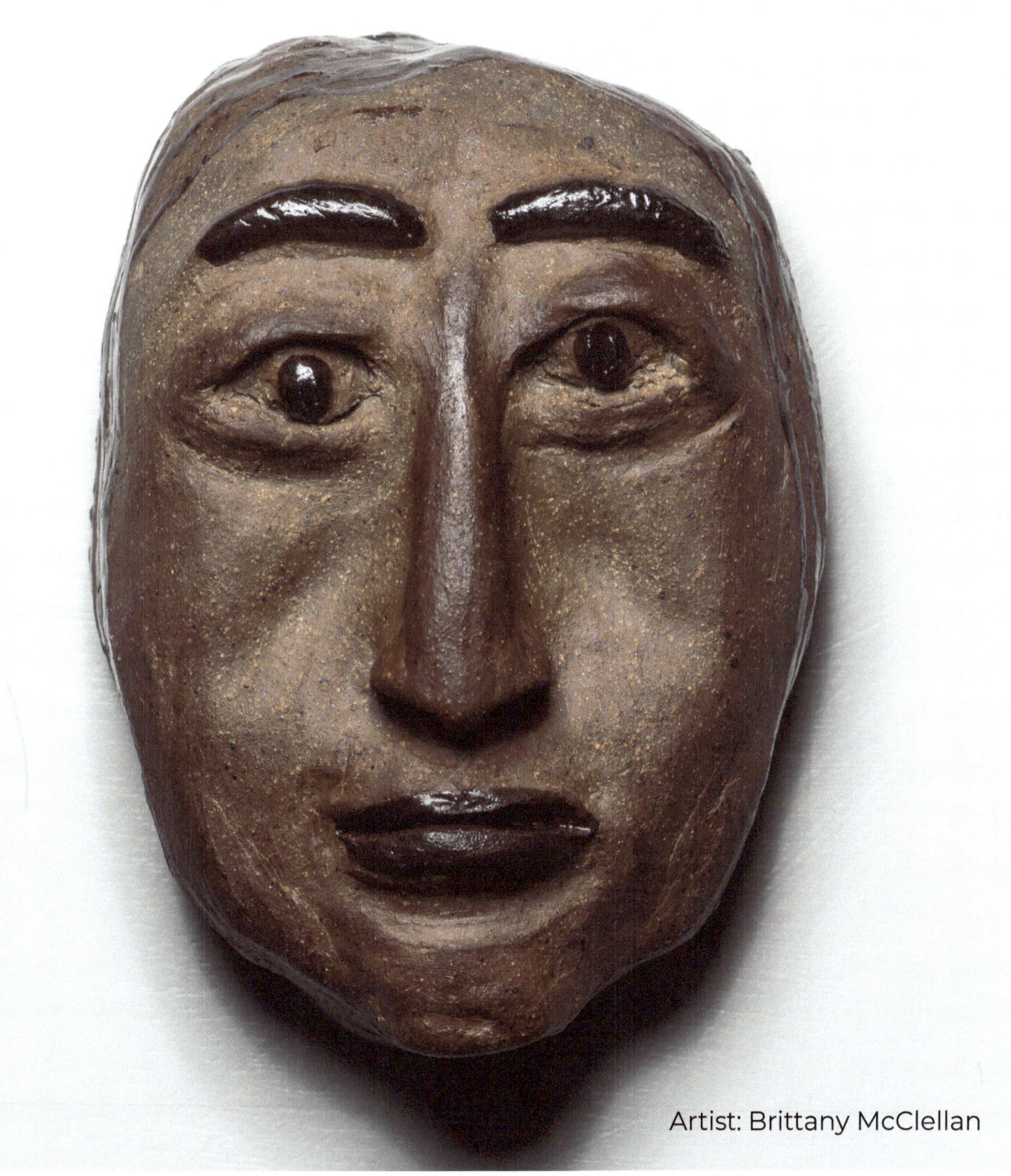

Artist: Brittany McClellan

Bob Garcia

A lucky man

Interviewed and nominated by Saskia de Rooy

I was born in this area but raised in Richland Center, Wisconsin with seven other brothers and three sisters. I was married once, but I was divorced. It was a good marriage, and I had two children out of my marriage. They're my life, kinda all I live for. My daughter is in San Antonio, Texas, and my son lives here in Waukesha with me. I have four grandchildren: two boys and two girls. I'm a lucky man. I was married to a woman named Rose. My ex-wife divorced me, and thirty years later, she came back here to Waukesha. She came to marry me, but she was a very ill woman. She had cancer, and I took care of her. Till the end. Just like she was my wife. She was here for three months, and then died. She came here to be with me, and I took care of her every night.

I was a maintenance man before, but I've painted for 35 years. I ended up in a nursing home doing painting and some light maintenance work, like groundskeeping. My plan was to be there for two or three months because I was afraid of the old folks. But 12 years went by… I just loved the elderly. I wish I could be there today… but something happened and the whole maintenance crew had to go. And then I ended up at Carroll University. That was an interesting story. I came here for an interview, and I hadn't walked ten steps away when they said, "Bob, you're hired." I was walking out the door, and someone said, "Bob, can you start Monday?" They knew I was a good painter. I had a good reference. And before that, I was a sandblaster, which is not an easy job: getting the dirt and rust off steel. You hold a hose and sand comes spraying out–little gold pellets, dit-dit-dit-dit against the steel. It would come out like a shiny table. It's very dirty work; we had to take two showers. It was good money, though.

I also listen to a lot of music, and I go to a lot of concerts. I sing while I paint, but no one notices. I'm a musician… I played the drums all my life. I played Rock and Roll, but not anymore. We had a bass player. He was killed in a snowmobile accident. He was riding on the lake, and he got kind of close to the edge, and he hit a tree stump, and he didn't see it. Boom. Off he went, and it killed him. I never played again. That's how much I loved him. The whole band never played again. It was a perfect band called Night Shift… everybody sold their equipment. That was one of the saddest days of my life. He was more than a friend. He was my brother-in-law, married to my sister, and one of the nicest guys I've ever met in my life. It can still bring a tear to my eye pretty easily. A good guy.

I've had a lot of sadness in my life because we have such a huge family. So I go to church as much as I can on Sundays, and I pray a lot. And I thank my God every day for what He has given me–which is life. I'm a guy that gets on my knees every day to pray. I don't just pray; I pray on my knees. It's funny when you do what we're doing–interviewing. What you find out about someone, isn't it? I'm the guy that likes to go and have fun. I'm outgoing. You can tell, right? But let alone the fun part, I am serious.

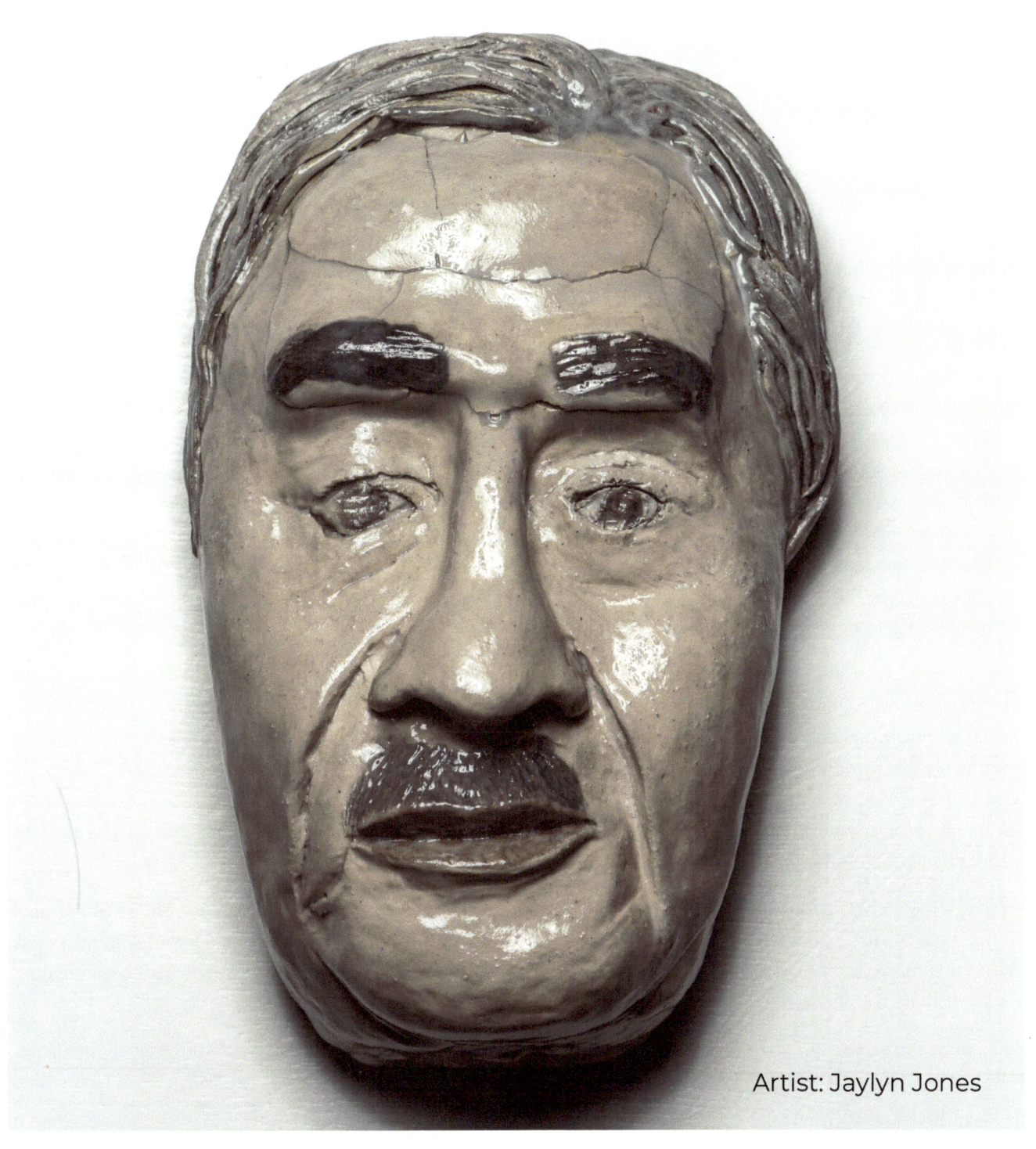

Artist: Jaylyn Jones

Wade Chamberlin
Seeing yourself evolve

Interviewed by Elizabeth Boziel, nominated by Kailey McDade

Growing up, I was an athlete up until senior year and then in college for a year. I usually would do three sports, so I didn't have much downtime; that was pretty much my life growing up. In high school I played football, wrestled, ran track, and played baseball–didn't do the best with my grades. I'm really passionate about fitness now because growing up, I got picked on a lot; I was this little fat kid and then… my freshman year I was 215-220 pounds. And sophomore year, I was still fat. And then between sophomore year and junior year, I decided, "All right, here's what we're gonna do." I just started working out a bunch, eating healthier. And now we're here. I'm lighter than I was freshman year and a lot bigger.

I came here to play football and do computer science. But then I quit football after sophomore after my freshman year, and now I'm a graphic design major. So it's a complete 180°. Changing my major gave me overall a more generally positive attitude towards school. I was originally computer science, [but] the math for that was way too much. So I switched to exercise science, and the chemistry was too much. So I switched to graphic design, which is what I initially wanted to do… The opportunities I was setting up for myself beforehand were not that great; I was getting bad grades and didn't understand the content. And then my girlfriend was saying, "You know you're really good at that stuff, I've seen you mess around with it, and you know what you're doing. Why don't you just try it?" I was worried, because I *enjoyed* graphic design, as a hobby. So I guess the "aha" moment was, "I can do this, and I'm going to enjoy the rest of my life way more if I do this now." My creativity has expanded a lot; that was always an important thing to me and now… I'm much happier…

One of my biggest life lessons is to not settle for mediocrity. The reason that anyone is successful is because they decided they weren't comfortable with the position they were at in life, and they did something about it. You know, you won't achieve anything by just sitting around and being complacent with where you are. It seems like people are forgetting to appreciate each other [and] treat each other with respect. You see all these crazy people that are doing crazy things, you can't help but think, What drove them to that? Did society fail them? I'm not religious or anything, but you can draw that from the Christian gospel: love your neighbor… Have morals; respect everyone. Sometimes, you've got to agree to disagree.

You know the conversation with gun control now? I'm a firm believer in the Second Amendment, and I know a lot of people here are not… that's just the demographic on campus, but… there's got to be some kind of change. I think it's sad that *this* is how conversation needs to be started, but the fact that now the conversation about gun control is started, that's a step forward in the right direction…

You can change…you can progress so much and evolve into…I wouldn't say a better person…but seeing yourself evolve into a *different* person–that, in my eyes, is a good thing. What's hard is knowing, "This isn't what I want,"…and not having the knowledge or means to change it.

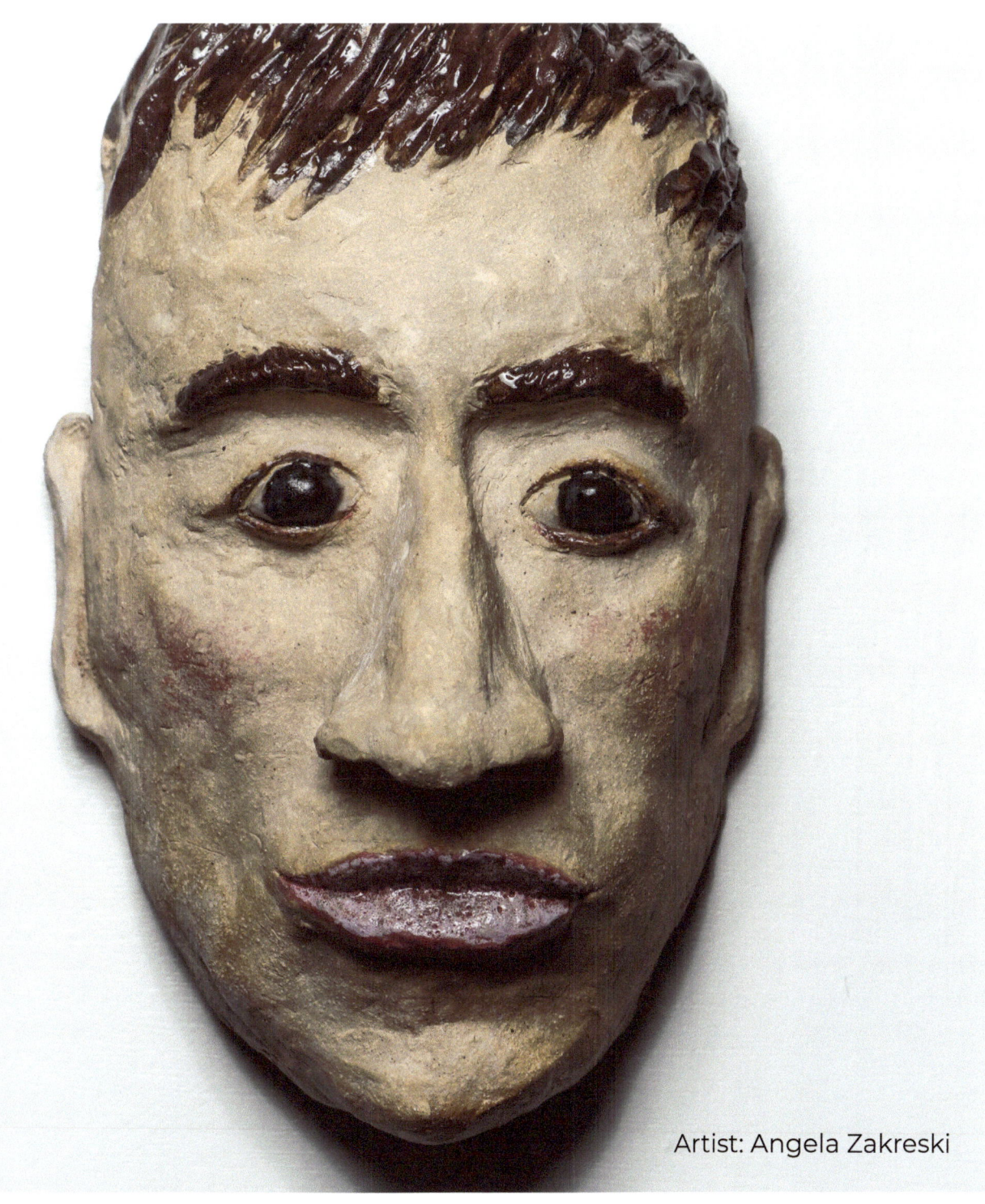

Artist: Angela Zakreski

Grant Wuerslin
You've just got to move

Interviewed by Griffin Idelman, Shea Carmichael, and Steven Grabowski,
nominated anonymously

There aren't many parts of me that went into Carroll that remained the same coming out of Carroll. My interest in music and video games and clothing remained the same. But the way I approach those things evolved pretty dramatically. I can still remember that specific conversation where I switched from just being a business major into getting the PPE degree.

Frankly, one of the best memories of Carroll was the fact that I was really able to use the cultural experience given to us as a way to truly step outside of my comfort zone and live my life more the way that I want to live, which is which mostly accounts to me creating stories and finding new experiences that I wouldn't have been able to find. With me basically having lived in Waukesha up until that point, I didn't really have the opportunity to jump into a city or jump into a whole new culture. As a whole, going to China the first semester of my junior year was a mind-blowing experience. It was a full semester of half hands-on, half hands-off guidance. We got a lot of direction early on, we had scheduled programing, a school trip, et cetera. But for a solid two and a half months, about three months, you're basically living your own life in a completely different city… I had enough space in order to jump out of my normal boundaries and really attempt to do something new with my life.

One thing I learned is that calculated stupidity will get you very far in this world. There's a lot of things I wouldn't have done if I had taken a second to think. Some of those ended up being bad, but a lot of them ended up being very, very good. And those are the things that I would not have had if I had thought too much; once you start thinking, you stop the ability to just move. Sometimes you've just got to move.

That's something I'm very happy about, that I basically moved my own way. I got my own internship with a mobile marketing firm, writing ad copy. I had all of these insane experiences—"truth is stranger than fiction" type experiences, because I was able to kind of muster up the courage to take that plunge and jump out of my comfort zone. And I think that if there's any sort of thing that I can say about advice for being at Carroll is take that leap, jump out of your comfort zone. That's how you truly grow. Because really, you know, life doesn't really get better; things don't get better. You just get better at dealing with them. I've learned to understand what I what I'm good at and a general sense of what I like to do. And generally the thing I try to do in life is take one or two of those things and put them together.

If it wasn't for Carroll, I might have taken safer options or taken less risk. And while the risks have not always paid out, the amount of happiness I've gotten from taking them has always been worth it.

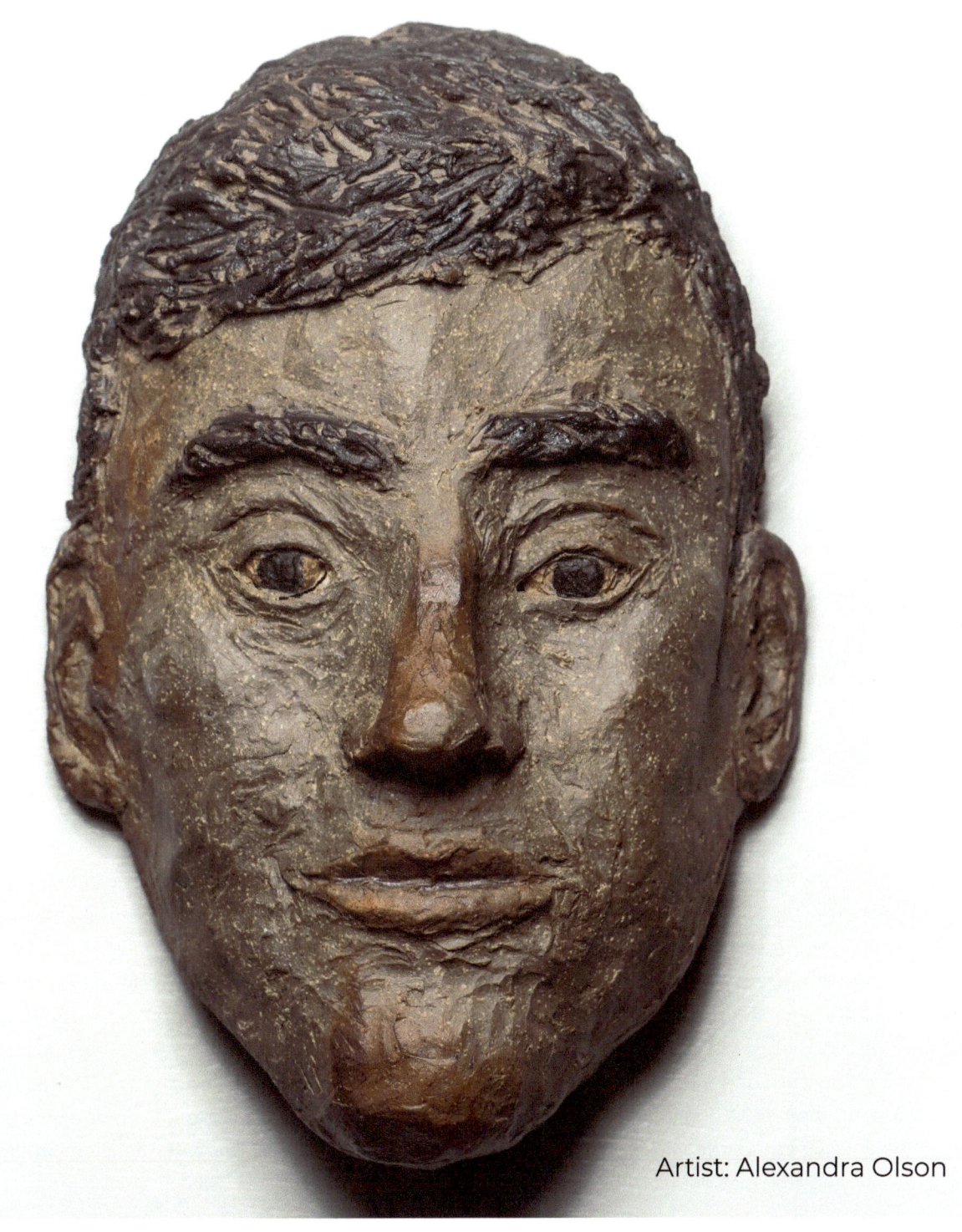

Artist: Alexandra Olson

Greg Gabrielsen
A huge gap

Interviewed by Mia Pham, nominated anonymously

When I took this job, I was in a transition period. I went to graduate school to get a PhD in physics, so I was going to be a researcher, a professor doing all kinds of groundbreaking work. And then… I tell the story to my students the first day of class: the semester before I changed my plan in grad school, I was working 20 hours a week in a laser optics lab. I was getting paid for it but hating every minute, and I was volunteering at night–teaching–and enjoying it. I had the realization I should find a way to flip these two things… The other job offer I sort of had when I accepted the position here was at a boarding school in Connecticut. I had never been to Connecticut. I've never been to boarding school. I do know a thing or two about teaching physics.

In grad school, there was a guy named Dr. Greg Francis who taught introductory physics. Watching him teach really helped me understand: the hardest part about being a physics teacher is recognizing that students, on the first day of Physics 101, don't know any physics, and you're a physics teacher. You've had years and years, decades of doing physics, so there's a huge gap between those two people. That's why so many people hate physics and hate science classes; you have geniuses teaching them, and they don't know a damn thing about what people who are brand-new are thinking.

I have learned a lot from my wife, recognizing that my own upbringing was not standard. I was born white, middle-class, male, straight, athletic, not disabled, all those kinds of thing, all those parts that I just take one hundred percent for granted because that's what I've been my entire life. Having met people, worked with people, taught people, I recognized that I can't assume that default for everybody. Realizing how many advantages in life I got without doing any work at all has made me a better person–a better teacher and a more complete person.

I have notions of getting into politics at some point in my life. My wife says there's not a chance; she doesn't want to be married to a congressman. I don't think I would even win an election but getting involved in that in some way shape or form, just trying to figure out more ways to contribute to the greater good. I think I teach because I get to help make other people "better" in some way, shape, or form. Any other ways I can help make the world a little bit better place, or a less awful place in some cases, would be something. I don't know exactly what form that takes just yet, but hopefully I'll be able to figure that out as time goes on. I'm concerned about all the things contributing to the further fracturing of political discourse in the country, in the world. More people getting their news and information from groups that are siloed [and] arguing their own truths as they define them. That, combined with technology, has made it easier for people with malicious intent… That is worrisome; trying to figure out how to how to fix that is not a simple task.

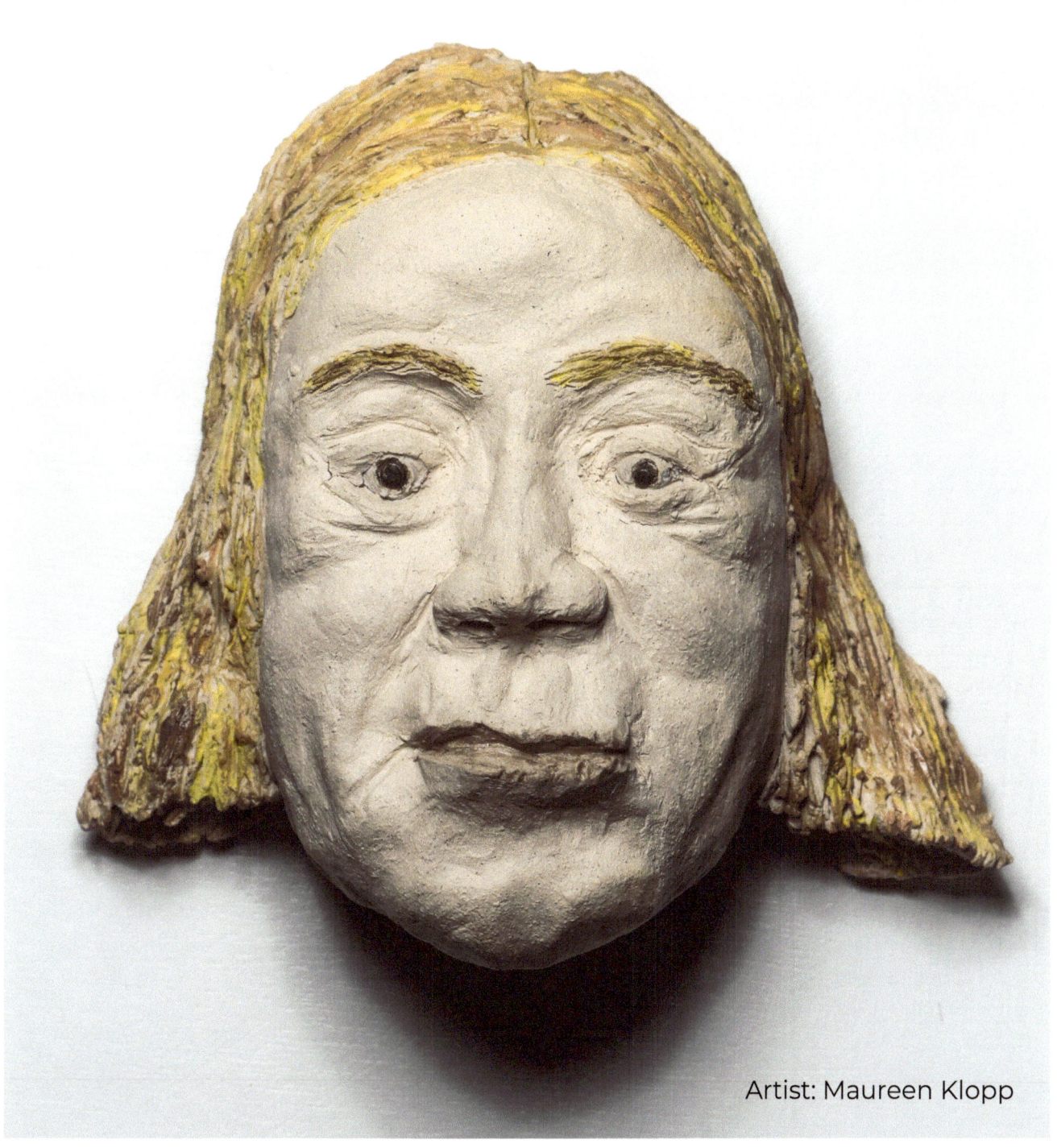

Artist: Maureen Klopp

Dan DeMerit

A lot like being a teacher

Interviewed by Emilie James, nominated by Jake Eisch

I grew up sledding on Lowell Hill here in Waukesha. I went canoeing on the Fox River; [I was] always playing sports, especially soccer as a kid. There's a unique history in Waukesha, you know, with all the different natural springs—that historically healthy water. I went to Summit View and Rose Glen for elementary school. Butler Middle School. Waukesha West High School. And from when I was a little kid going to sports camps and swimming lessons to now running those things—being a part of other people's recreation is a fun thing. Rec sports at Carroll is a lot of things: intramurals, club sports, the facilities where people work out, equipment check out, the cheer and the dance team. I'm the only professional staff overseeing all that.

I think we have a strong educational system and good schools, and both my parents were teachers, so to be in an educational environment falls right in line with what I always wanted to do. My whole family—everyone's Phys Ed teachers. Physical Education—gym class—was a really cool thing for me growing up. My dad was a gym teacher at Whittier Elementary just down the road from Waukesha South High School; he also worked at Butler and Waukesha South, coaching and doing things like that. He really got that from his parents; both of them were physical education teachers. The DeMerit family has multiple-sport college athletes, people who lived that athletic life, whether at the high school level or college level. They were always teaching others and became some of the first coaches. My grandma was one of the first women female coaches in the state of Wisconsin…I look up to the kind of person who enjoys being around other people and making them better. So that's something that I try to do and bring into my work as well. In my world, coaches, certain teachers I've had, family members, athletes… that's where I look for my motivations.

[At UW-La Crosse], I really connected with business and sports and found this relatively new initiative within higher education: Rec Sports—Campus Recreation. Colleges and universities have to have a place for people to work out; sometimes that's a formal class where people are learning how to do a sport, and other times it's a more informal kind of education. I know that you all as students are obviously here for academics. But there's a lot outside of the classroom… you need to know how to be a healthy person.

Without actually being a teacher myself, this is a lot like being a teacher at an institution of higher education. It's not a curriculum necessarily; it's a little more informal, and yet it's what people do for the rest of their lives, whether for fun or just to stay healthy. That's something that I've found to be passionate about.

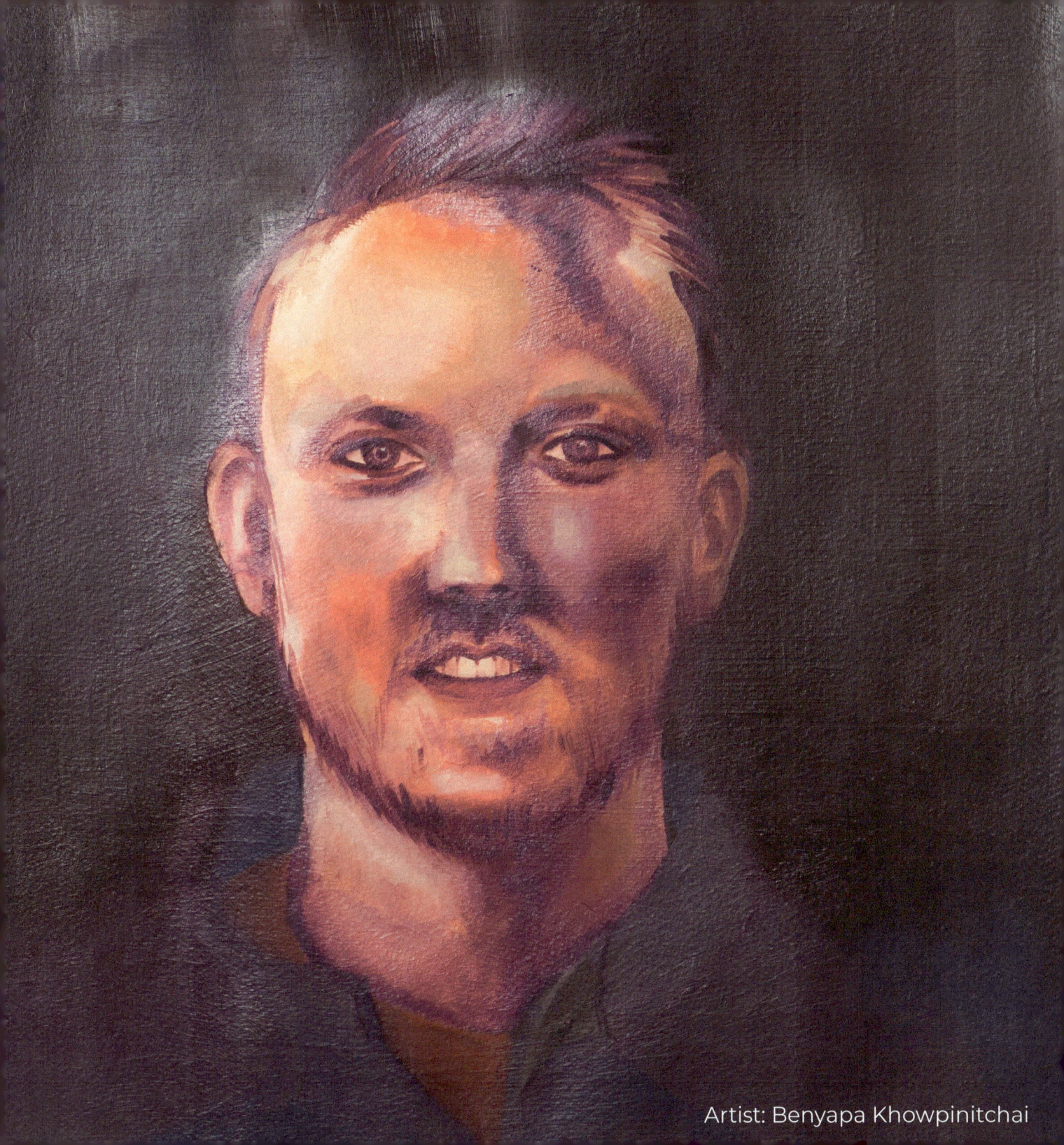

Artist: Benyapa Khowpinitchai

Sarah Stock
But keep your mind open

Interviewed by Caleb Beres, Ronald Dignadice, and Steven Grabowksi,
nominated by Travis Neils

I came to Carroll in part because it was close to home… The other part was that it was kind of my dream school, if you want to call it that. I remember being a little kid and my mom driving past the school, and I was thinking how cool it was and how I wanted to end up there some day.

I double majored in biology and professional writing with a biochemistry minor and a pre veterinary emphasis… I've always been super passionate about animals. I'm in veterinary school right now. And I was passionate about arts and theater and writing and the more creative side. I liked that Carroll had a little bit of everything.

Professor Best over in the writing department was probably the most influential person that I met at Carroll because he really pushed me to explore writing and to continue becoming a better writer, which ultimately inspired me to take on the professional writing major. I continue pursuing that even now as a freelance public writer. So it's not only been something that gives me a lot of fulfillment but has also helped fund my way through vet school. Dr. Schneider in the biology department was also a super huge help. She helped make biology classes interesting, and now that I'm in vet school, I can see that she really laid a good foundation for the classes I've encountered. She was good at distilling concepts down to the bones—what's important, what you need to know, and what are the details you really have to hold in your mind. She made complex subjects not seem so hard to grasp.

I was also an actor at Carroll. I was in "Heathers: The Musical, "Legally Blond," "Numbers Nerds," which is also a musical and… and then I came back as an alum and was in "Almost Mame." Every production was a lesson in teamwork, recognizing that you rely on other people to say their lines, and they rely on you to say your lines… So you have a duty to perform well for the sake of helping other people perform well. But at the same time, if something goes wrong, you should also be prepared to step in and help; don't leave them hanging out there.

Otherwise, I worked with another student to start the Pre-Vet club… I'm glad we helped start something that's still around. And at the end of the day, that's really all we wanted to do, [although] it maybe would have been nice to feel like we had a fully functional club up and running versus quick trying to find someone to carry the torch so it didn't implode.

With any creative project, it's just difficult sometimes to… keep focus. Coming up with new ideas and developing those new ideas instead of getting distracted by a new idea. Just trying to stick with one thing… but keep your mind open to the way that projects change and evolve. In a year or so, I'll hopefully be finding a job in a small animal, general practice clinic. Once I get settled in and have everything kind of under control there, then I hope to keep up with writing as more of a passion project and just see where that takes me.

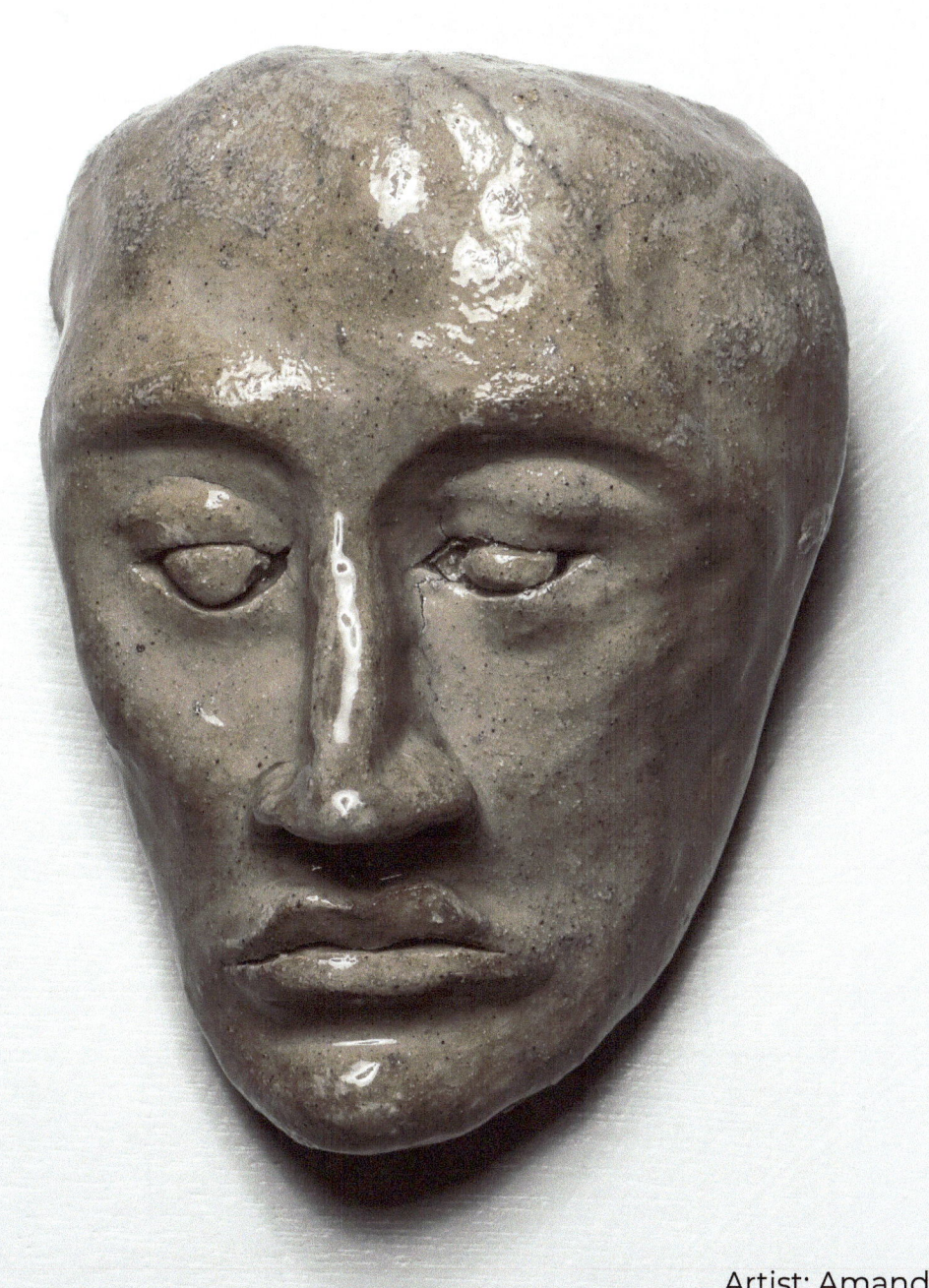

Artist: Amanda Zarder

Thitikan Thianjan

Expectations

Interview by Corey Kowalski and Cassidy Neefe, nominated by Amy Cropper

I came [to the United States] spring break of seventh grade, and the first couple weeks of school… I had no idea what people were saying. I only knew the basics, like "Hi, how are you?" "Good, thank you." And that's it. Literally that's it. Just ABCs. I just kind of learned by looking at other people…

A lot of tourists are going to Thailand now, to the touristy places… But where I came from, there weren't a lot of tourists and foreigners. We do learn English. The school that I went to [is] a Catholic school, a private school, so we had three language requirements: Thai, English, and Chinese. But they just focused on cramming the material into your brain; they forget that too much information just doesn't work for students. Teachers over here [are] more forgiving. They help you a lot. They're really helpful. They're like God's son: they can help you with anything. In Thailand, we have some kind of power distance… it's like… By asking your teacher a question, you're basically challenging them to see if they know the subject matter. They view it that way, but over here, it's more like if we ask a question, we mean we don't understand it. We want to gain knowledge from the professor because they know more than us. It's the opposite over there: if we ask a question, they basically say, "I just gave everything to you…. I just gave all the information to you. Why don't you retain it, learn it?" You're not supposed to ask a question because it's seen as challenging them; you're not supposed to challenge their power…

The most important person in my life is my mom because she brought me here. She's been living here for ten years, and then six years ago she decided, "Hey, I've settled myself down. Why don't I just bring my daughter here to get educated, learn a second language and such?" My aunt, she's the one that raised me through all my childhood, and she said, "Yes, it would be good for you too." [I really had] no choice but to come here because basically, my mom and my aunt had already decided. I was both nervous and excited. "What are people going to be like? They're going to hate me. Are they going to like me? Am I going to be the oddball in school? Do you guys write in cursive?" It's many different emotions combined. "Are people really going to like me? Are they going to look at me weird?" But surprisingly…. they were really friendly, especially the boys; they got excited more than anybody, jumping in front of me, like "Hiii! My name is …" And I'm like, "Okaaay… Nice to meet you too."

In Thailand, everyone follows the group; we are more collectivist…When you do something outside your group, they look at you: "What are you doing? Are you crazy? Why are you acting so weird?" Over here, you can just act however you feel; you're free to express your opinion… [If I could do it over], I wouldn't have watched so many American movies, because it's just the stereotype of America: how American people act, what they do… especially mean girls. Really mean girls. I literally expected every high school to be like that, with girls who are mean to everybody, *everybody*. My friends say to me all the time, "If people make fun of you, you just ditch them… just ignore them." But I think it's the opposite. You have to approach people first, get to know them, rather than just ignore them.

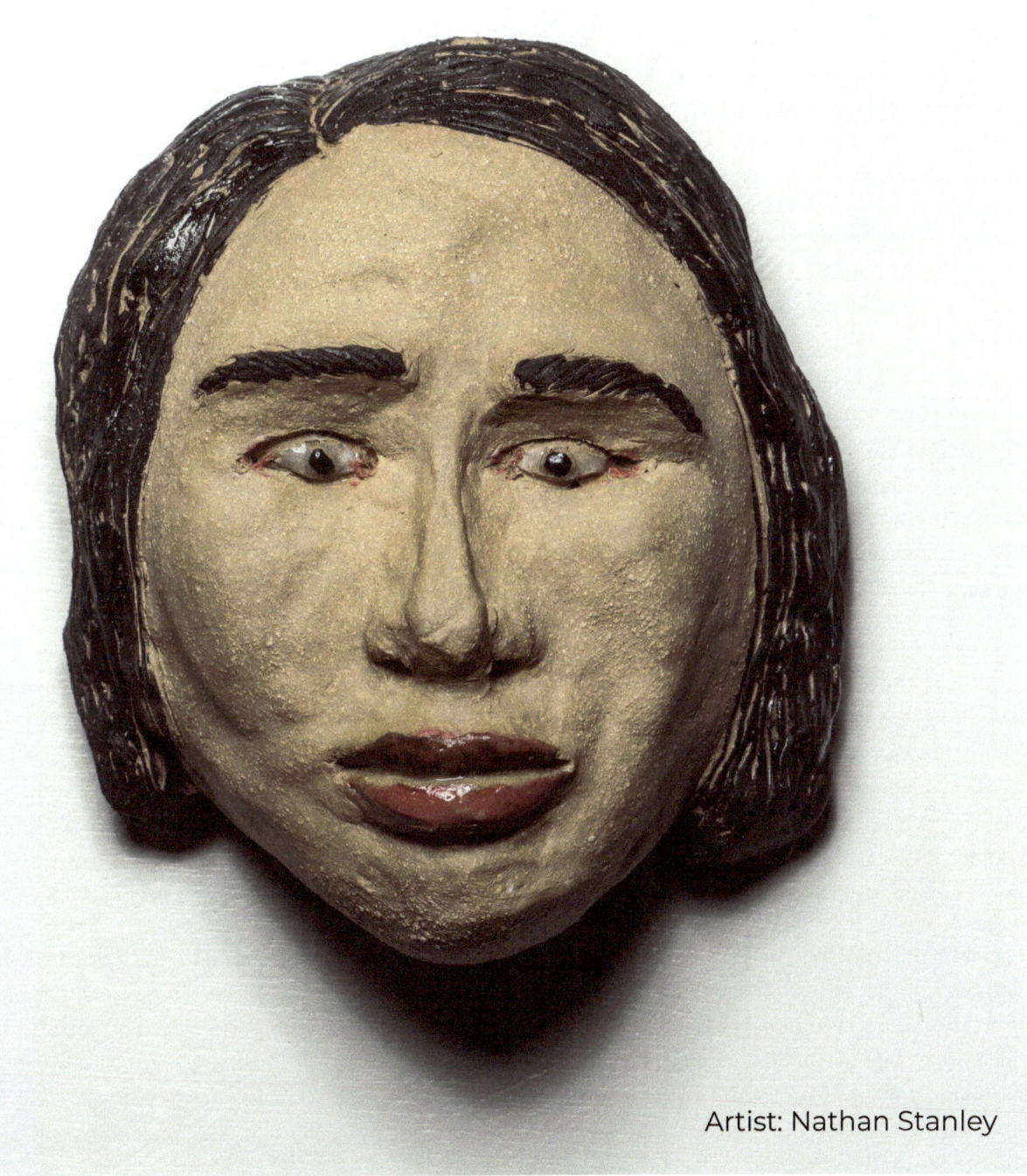

Artist: Nathan Stanley

Rachael Verhoef
Gauge it for yourself

Interviewed by Hannah Savage-Cooper, Alex Straszewski, and Steven Grabowski, nominated by Isabella Ruggiero

When I was thinking about college, I had about 36 majors that I liked. I had a really hard time narrowing it down. I was thinking about social work or political science. Maybe gender studies... When I studied abroad for my Communication major, I took a gender and sexuality class that I really adored. So I think in another life, on another timeline, I would have been a gender and sexuality scholar, because I think the perception of who you are as a person and your sexuality defines a lot of who you are.

And then I thought to myself, "Wow, I want to be so many things. What can help you be all of those things in one lifetime? Acting can." There are opportunities. You just have to work hard to get them. A lot of people say things like, "You're going into the theater arts. What are you going to do, live in a box?" And yeah, it's a lot of work. It's a lot of work. And if people aren't willing to do the work, you won't succeed. But I think it was James Zager who told me that half, even most, of being an actor is being a hard worker. And being resilient. That stuck with me; he said that you need to be able to get pushed down and come back up again. And I can do that. I've been doing it my whole life. Push me down; I'll just get back up. That's a big aspect of the arts. People are just so resilient... And that's why we need the arts. Having artists and people who are willing to... sacrifice a lot of luxury, and willing to power through, those are really important to political change, social change, too, I think. And people lose sight of that often... yes, it helps us forget about hardship... and it also can bring about change... it's all-encompassing.

And I just love acting. Throughout my whole life, that's been something that I've always come back to. I'm fascinated by all the individual people, the individual stories... I think that's one of the reasons that I'm a performer. I love the pieces that come from different parts of history, different classes of people, too. That there are horrible, heart-wrenching stories and also stories of survival. Honestly, everything that I have done in my life. All the mistakes that I've made, friends that I've lost, friends that I've gained, relationships that I've had, relationships that I've lost, places I've traveled, all those things have added up to me being here in this moment, so you can have regrets and a will to want to do things over. But in the end, you can't. And I think the most important thing as a human, looking back on the past, is not to dwell on it, but to learn from it and move forward.

Success is different to everyone. You have to gauge it for yourself. It can be little things. For some people, it's overcoming mental health issues or overcoming old trauma. For some people, it's getting that big job. For others, like artists, it's getting a part time job at Starbucks but also teaching, doing acting jobs on the side... Success can be little things. It can be really big things. I think what a lot of people are losing is that not everyone can be super successful right away. And it's OK if you aren't. You can't judge yourself based on other people who have had different advantages and disadvantages than you had. Your successes will be different than others. And that's OK.

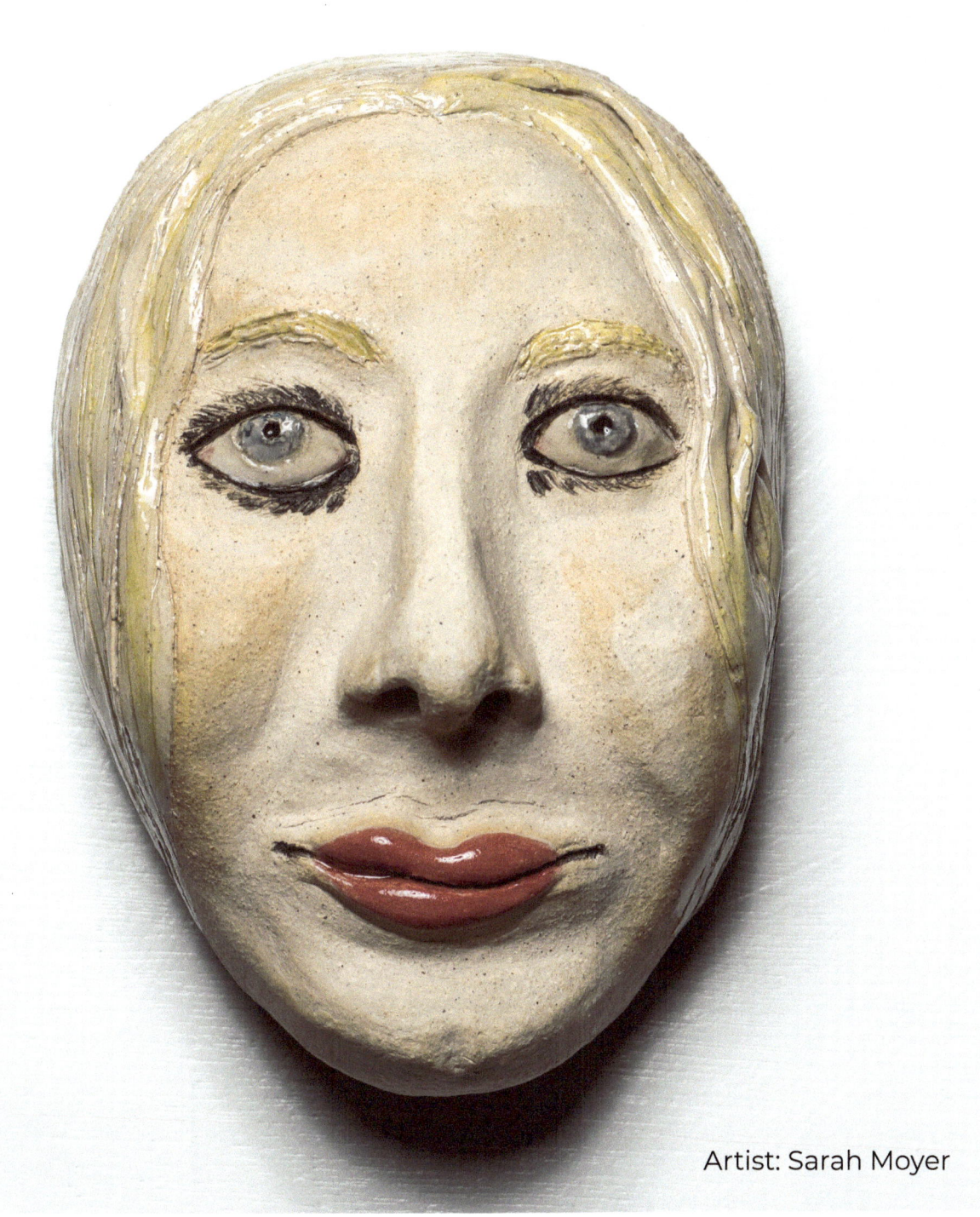

Artist: Sarah Moyer

Amanda Collette

A bridge

Interviewed by Emily Poffinbarger, nominated anonymously

I'm a caretaker for a boy with Autism. I babysat for years, but it's not nearly as rewarding as being a caretaker, especially a population that is so ostracized and so diminished. It's hard for people to treat individuals with Autism like people; it is. Sometimes I even find it hard to not talk to him as you would a little kid. He's a freshman in high school, and he's going through one of the hardest stages in his life. It's emotional to see someone at their worst 24/7. And even when they are at their best, people don't recognize that it *is* their best. It's hard to realize that. It takes a certain person with a certain heart to have the patience to want to work with someone who has such severe cognitive and physical disabilities but is such a lively person inside. He's the funniest kid ever; he just can't find the words to say it.

I feel like a bridge between him and the rest of the world; he can experience things, not necessarily through his own eyes all the time, because he can't, but through mine as well. I can share with him what goes on out there and things that he can't see himself. Not all people should have the desire to do that, but they *should* have a desire to make a difference in someone's life. It's not necessarily helping others because I've found—all over North and South America—that people don't want to be helped; they want to know that there's someone out there who cares about them.

I feel like they always deserve to have someone there for them, whether it's a phone call away or someone on the opposite side of the globe or your next-door neighbor. To have someone that's always there for you no matter what, with whatever you might need, if it's a natural disaster or if it's you have an ingrown toenail and you need someone to pluck it out. When I've traveled, that's all I look for at this point. I can't tell you how many times I've wanted that—someone to lean in, to say, in the way they want, that I'm here for you.

I want to base my life in social justice, especially within the immigrant community… I've never been through that myself, but I know people who are going through it as I talk right now. It's hard. It is. I have this weird passion for minority rights and especially immigrants, people who have been put in situations that they did for the sake of their family, or for the sake of themselves or for the sake of their rights, and so on. They literally give up their rights as a person to get their necessities. I think about what Cesar Chávez did—the forty-day fast or something. He made such a difference in a community that is so overlooked, even though it makes up like a quarter of our population. It's not even just about immigrants from Mexico and Latin America, but all over the world. He changed the lives of millions and millions of people and is still changing them today even though he's… he can't anymore. He made a move that people will never forget, *can't* forget, because now it's a *right*. It's a human right to have working conditions that are suitable—not as an American citizen, but as a *person*.

I've been told for a long time by my boyfriend to stop *saying* things and just to start *doing* them. It's really impacted me. I mean, I've always thought, "Why don't you be an activist or an advocate for someone?" But I don't just want my voice to be heard; I want my actions to be understood. And for there to be a purpose for what I'm doing. I want my actions to live through other people. I want people to just continue on.

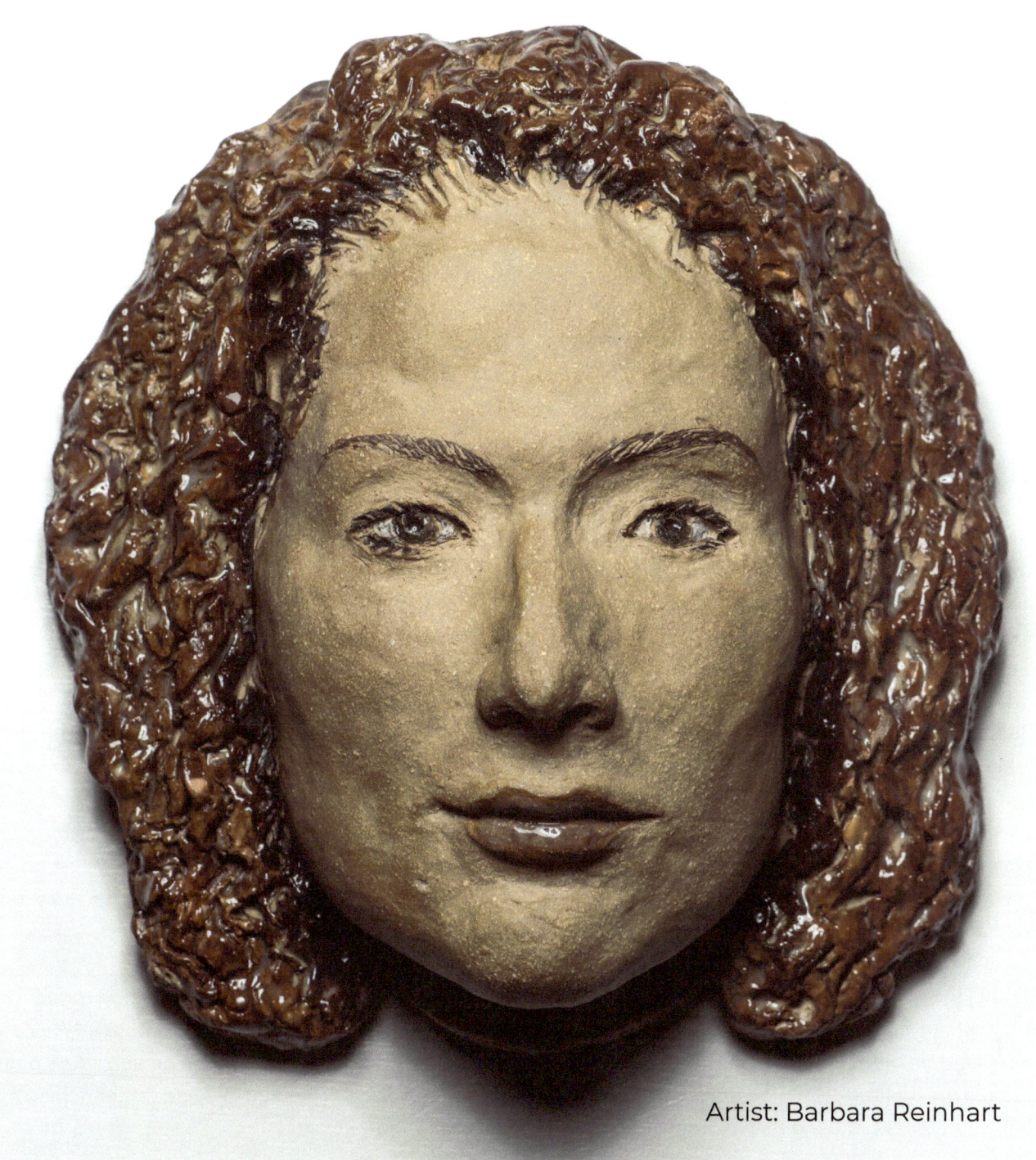

Artist: Barbara Reinhart

Maggie Treants

Get past your fear

Interviewed by Alyssa Polewaczyk and Desirae Dunn, nominated anonymously

I was homeschooled from kindergarten to third grade. I don't really remember why… [Just] because, I think, both my parents worked from home. And then I went into middle school—in a really small town, really small school. I did not fit in there at all… It's funny looking back on it, because people think it's such a sad story, but I look at it now… I had very few close friends in middle school there, [and] when I wasn't hanging out, I just kind of dove into art and music; I spent all my time doing that. …And so basically, whenever I felt like I was not belonging somewhere, I would just work on stuff. And I've learned to just keep doing that in college; that's all I know how to do, really… I'm actually kind of thankful because if I had been socially active and had a huge social life, running around with people all the time, or I was never home and never had time to create, I wouldn't be as skilled at certain things as I am now. So I wouldn't say I'm thankful for being bullied, but I'm thankful that I was able to cope with it in a way that was productive and healthy.

Now that I've started to branch out and travel, I'm like, "I need to get out of small towns." Carroll's a nice step-pingstone, but now I've got to go. My wings are spread, I've got to fly! I just want to find a place where I belong in a way, whether that's in the US or Australia or who knows; I don't know. Somewhere I can just authentically be myself without feeling guilty for it because that's…been the result of bullying: I felt guilty for liking certain things and not growing up the conventional way. I just want to find a niche. I like being able to be myself and like the things I like. I don't have to make a bunch of money but just live sustainably while still being able to do stuff I like. And have cats. At a minimum. I mean, yeah, I'd like a partner in the future, but I'll take cats, for the time being.

The thing that's keeping me here is my family: my dad, my mom, and my grandma… I know my grandma with Alzheimer's doesn't have that much time. So I'm going back home this summer for a few months… because I want to see her more. And my dad has ongoing health issues; things could happen literally any time. And my mom… they're older, so I am worried about that as well. I sometimes feel I have this obligation to stay for them, especially because I've seen my dad take care of my grandma so well. Even though my dad says, "Just go, go do what you want with your life. We're going to support you doing that. Don't feel like you need to stay, take care of us and stuff."

[I know] there's going to be a point when I can't sustainably keep staying here and not progressing myself—not doing what I want just because I'm living in fear. You can't constantly hold yourself back and say, "Well, this could happen or this could happen," or "I don't want that to happen," or "I'm afraid of this person who's going to make me feel bad," …If you don't get past your fear, you're never going to actually have an enriching life. That was a really big thing that hit home for me when I was really young.

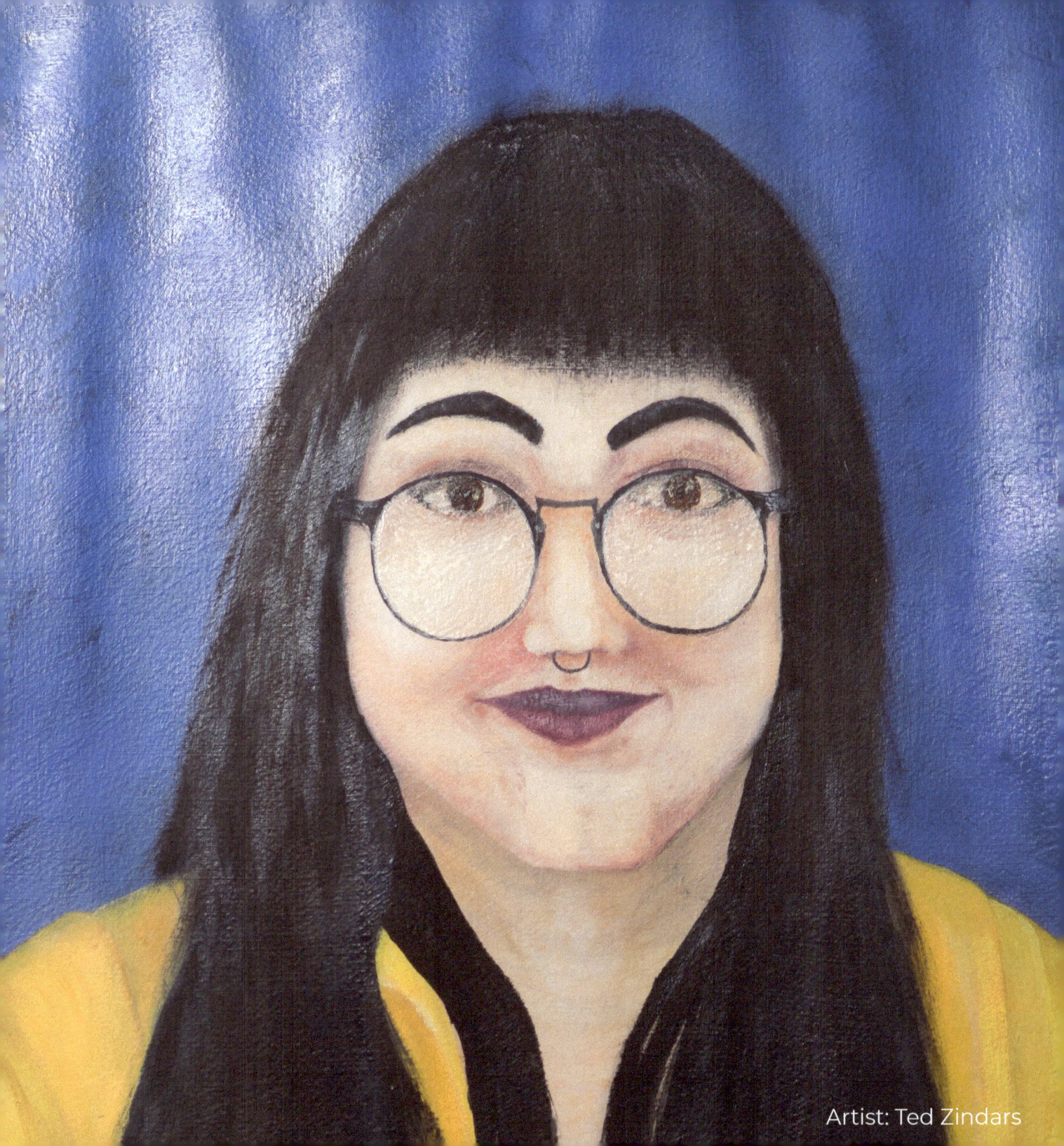

Artist: Ted Zindars

Hannah Prosser

This is my life

Interviewed by Clara Clifford, nominated by Cassidy Levenhagen

My mom threw me into dance at age three. I liked it, had a good time in the studio, never tried to rebel out of it. I started with ballet and tap, and then everything else came later. And I'm still dancing; I'm on Blaze [Carroll's dance team]. So I got into [that] as a freshman. I was shocked: "Oh, I got it! I can't believe I made this team!" It was a really weird transition. I was so overwhelmed when we were learning the audition poms routine; I'd never held a pom in my life. And this style—everything was sharp and tight. In studio dance, you can't be stiff.

We perform at football and basketball games and do extra exhibitions in the area… We host Spirit of Hope, which raises money for breast cancer research. I've been a team captain since my sophomore year. I run stretching. I do all the music: cut everyone's songs, burn the CD, change the tempos, whatever. I have learned how to talk to people better, because I feel like prior to this, my communication skills were kind of crappy. You have to be nice to your team… but you also have to be hard on them… It's that balance…

…I was in a car accident when I was a sophomore in high school and was wheelchair bound for a while. I broke everything, and the doctors told me I should not dance again. I was like, "Screw you, guys!" I was in my wheelchair, then on crutches when I started to go to class, and then I was in a boot; it was a horrible six-month span of my life. I was determined to get back into dance. The following year they said, "Never do *en pointe* (toe shoes) again." They were firm on that. But… I'm the kind of person who will do what I want. So the year after that, I did an *en pointe* solo recital just to prove to myself…. My ankle had gotten two screws in it… but I was trying to prove to myself that I can still do this if I want to. I was determined to do this *en pointe* solo—and I did it, and it was great. I never did *en pointe* after that, but I just had to prove it to myself. This is my life. If I don't do it, what's my point here? I can't even imagine not dancing.

Dancing has taught me to be a team player, too, because you can't be like, "Ok, *I'm* going to do this." You have to get your whole team to want the same thing… I'll say, "I know I can't do this skill for the life of me, but I know what it's supposed to look like." I can tell people what they're doing wrong, and they can say the same thing [for me].

I'm actually moving to Texas after I graduate. I want to be a Dallas Cowboys cheerleader. So we (me and my boyfriend) are going to stay there for five years, and I'll work my way onto that team… It's going to be rough… but I'm pretty determined to do it. I'm totally planning on it taking me three tries to even make it past the first stage [auditions]. I'm just focusing on dance the next two years and then hopefully [pursue forensic psychology] and still dance. I have my work cut out for me.

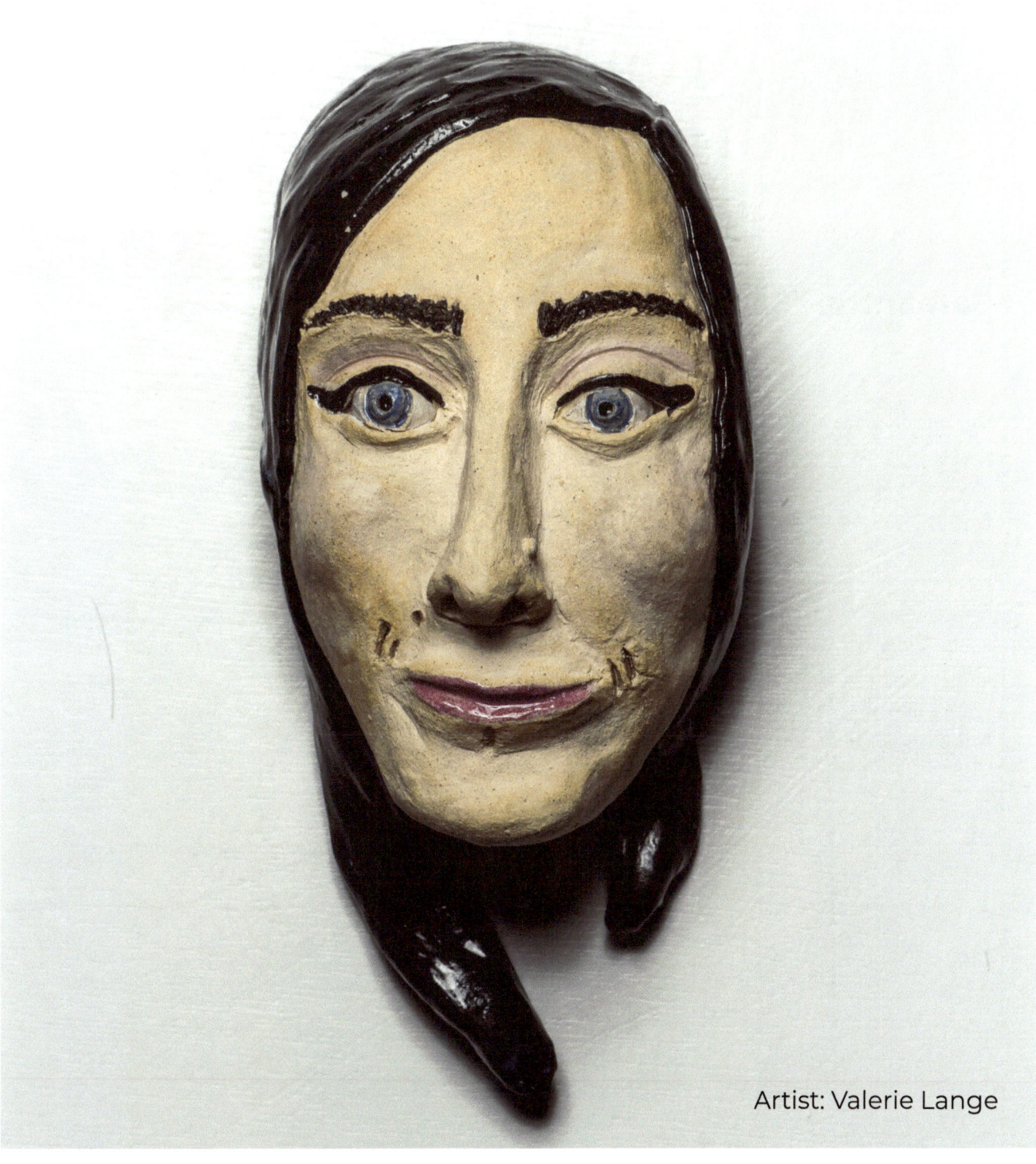

Artist: Valerie Lange

Samantha "Sami" Seybold

Samantha has a unique educational upbringing. Being digitally schooled allowed Samantha to focus on her studies without being distracted by public schools' traditional curriculum. During her younger years, she was involved in her church's "Girls Club," which allowed her to find a social outlet and grow in her faith. She began to understand the ideas of feminism and became a strong advocate for equal rights. Arriving at Carroll, Samantha was quite nervous about the idea of going to college due to her lack of understanding what the traditional classroom would be like. Once Sam arrived, she flourished on campus: being involved in clubs, growing in her faith, and excelling in her classes. Samantha has chosen to pursue additional education after Carroll, hoping to attend grad school in California for philosophy. Her goal is to serve God and make the world a better place through spreading kindness to others. Her wish is to guide others in respecting themselves and knowing their self-worth. Sam hopes to one day become a professor and teach young adults these ideas in order for them to flourish in life the way she feels she has had the opportunity to do at Carroll.

Introduced by Taylor Dlapa, Jessie Lehmann, and Anna Redding, nominated anonymously

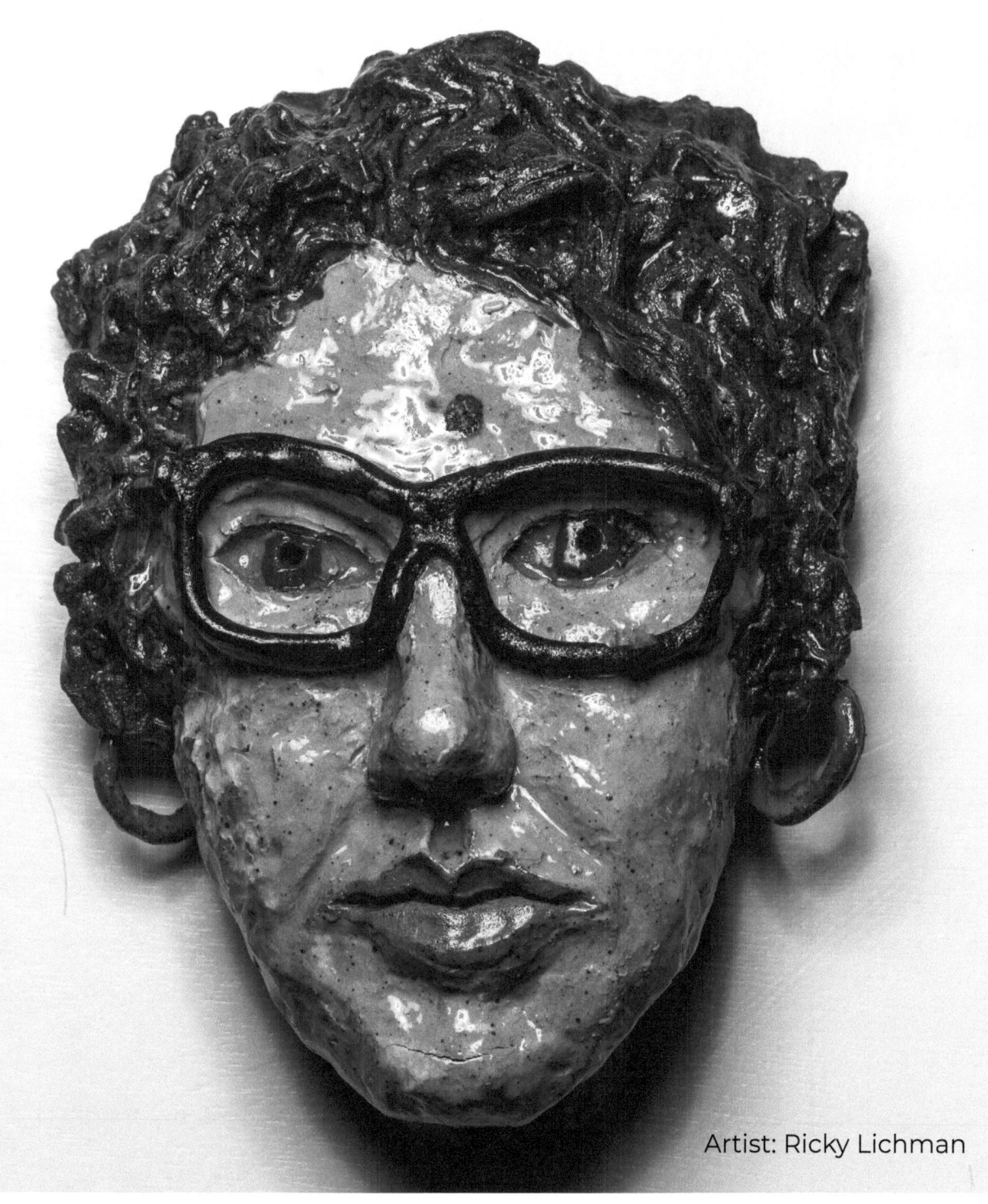

Artist: Ricky Lichman

Tlaloc Huera

One of Tlaloc's defining values is his passion for indigenous people. As a Mexican-American deeply embedded in two different cultures, he knows firsthand the power dynamics between cultures. Tlaloc brings that awareness to his coursework, which complicates our understanding of Spanish colonization of the Americas. Bartolome de Las Casas and Juan Gines de Sepulveda, for example, both justified colonization, but only de Las Casas demanded that indigenous people be treated with respect and dignity. In his Capstone, Tlaloc analyzed how the indigenous people of Mexico infused the image of the Virgin of Guadalupe with a defiant spirit of resistance. Tlaloc shares that bold spirit through his own words, actions... and music. Yes, besides double majoring in Psychology and Religion, supporting youth with Autism, and playing soccer, Tlaloc is also an amazing musician; not surprisingly, his music empowers and promotes justice for those with less power in today's society.

Introduced by Jim Grimshaw, nominated by Sara Meyer

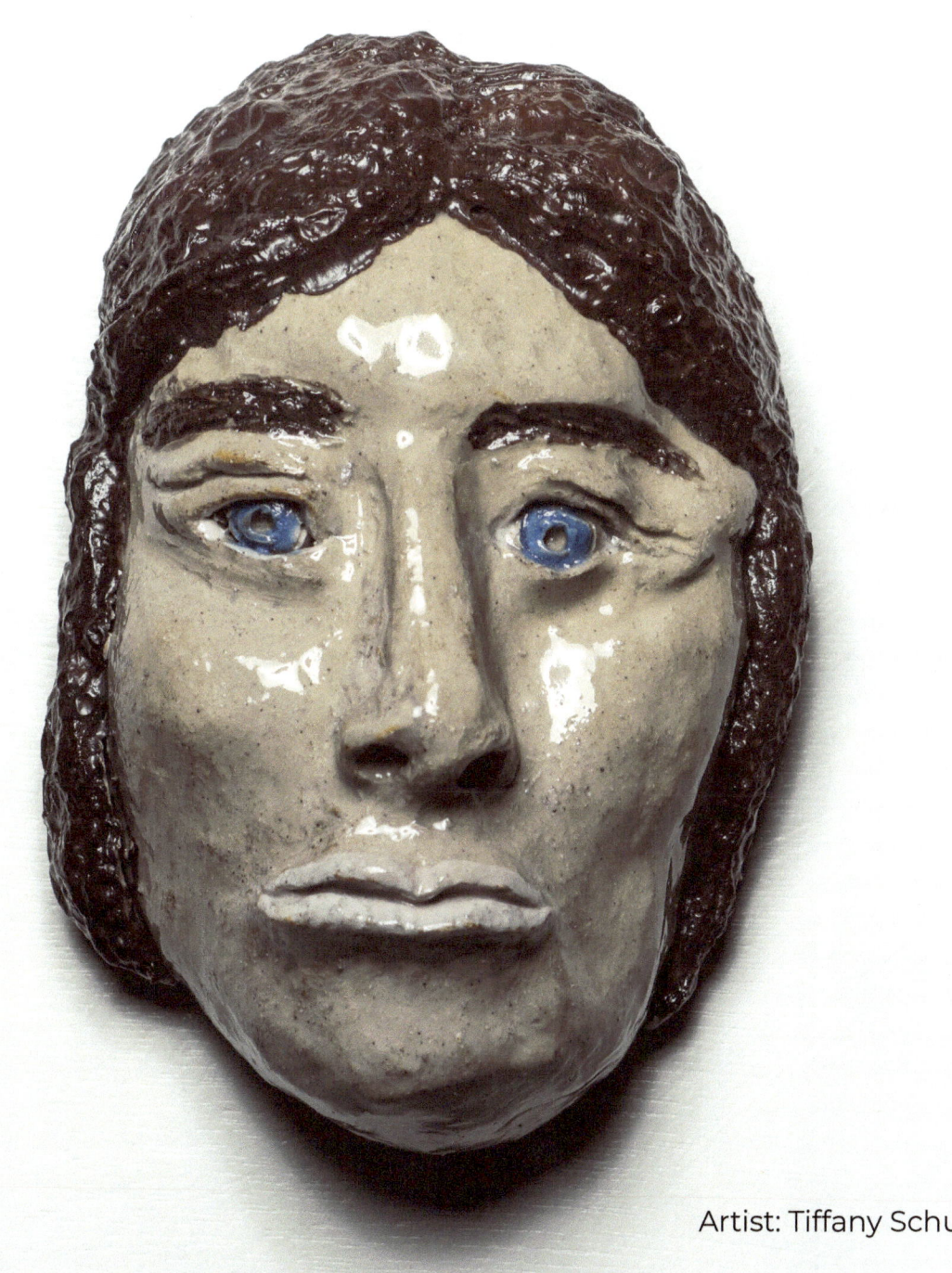

Artist: Tiffany Schutte

Kelly Pringle

"I'm an environmentalist. Honestly, people have been asking me why I got into it, and I don't really know what drove me to it. When I was in high school, we had projects that required us to pick a topic to talk about, and I was always drawn to this specific subject. It's sad what is happening within the environment, and I realized that nothing was going to get done about it, so it pushed me to become an environmental science major. When I originally started in school, I wasn't even involved in the environmental field at all. I actually wanted to be a marine biologist. I realized after about a year at Carroll that I didn't want to intern in Hawaii for marine biology; I wanted to stay in Wisconsin and make a difference in the world on an environmental level. So many professors have changed the way I see things from an environmental perspective and have really helped me develop my interests in this particular field, and I want to share it with others."

Interviewed by Brittany Drag, nominated by Kent Earl

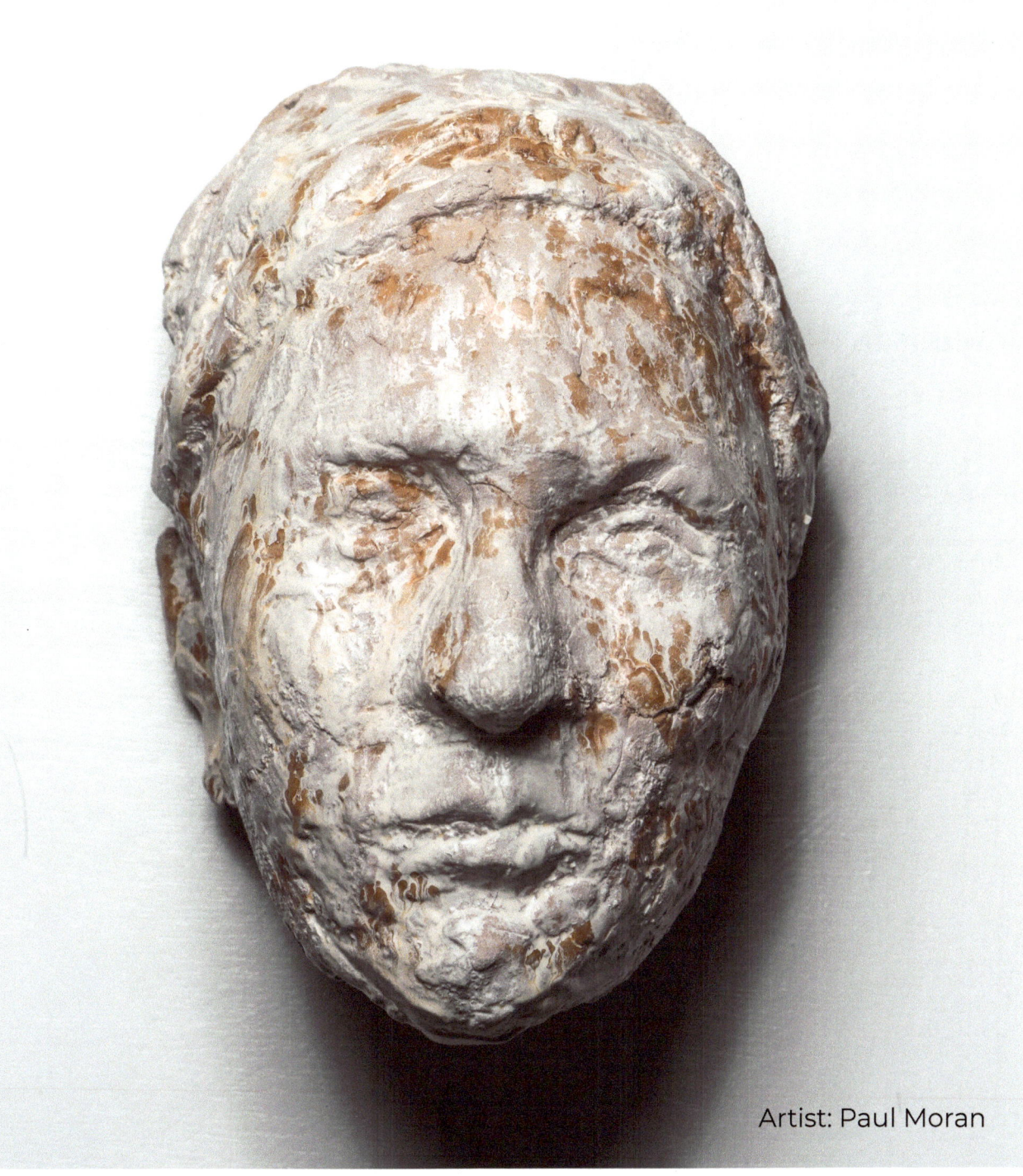

Artist: Paul Moran

Melissa Palacios

Because I am first generation, my parents do not have the same experience as me. I've had to be independent, ask for help, resources, and push myself. Helping other first-generation students is my motivation; it's why I became a mentor. I've learned to communicate with them differently. I am a very curious person, so I ask about their families or school, if they have any worries. They usually open up to me, and I always try to help them… Since everything is new to them, I tell them they have to get used to it, put themselves out there… I love that they still come back to me, asking for help with classes, even becoming mentors themselves. A lot of people who know me say I give them hope… they see I'm doing good because I always try to make the best of my experiences. Live up your life, explore, try new things… be happy doing what you are doing despite what other people think.

Interviewed by John Serrano, nominated by Jasmine Palacios

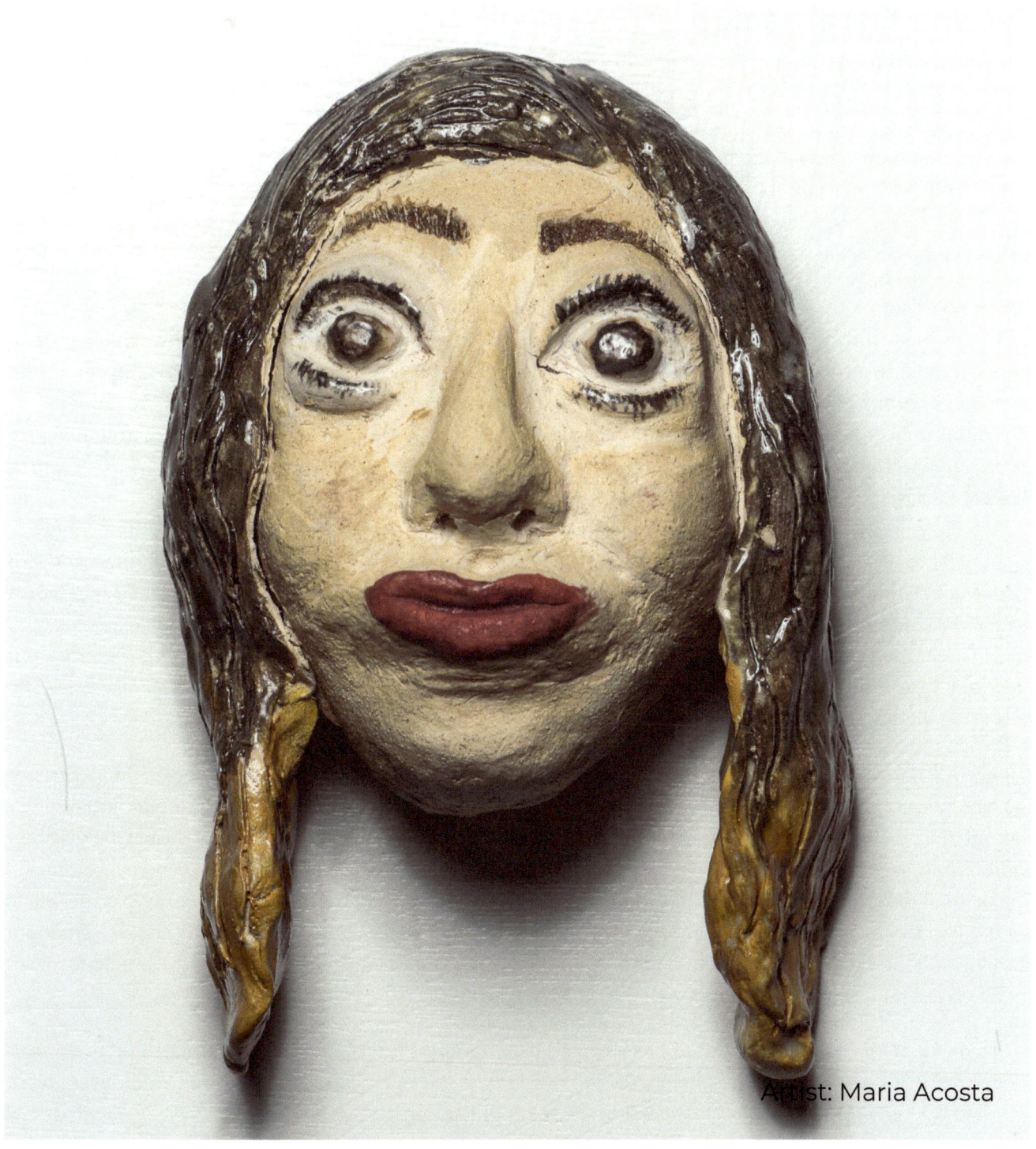

Artist: Maria Acosta

Czarina Encarnacion
Just go with it

Interviewed by Loey Dodge and Steven Grabowski, nominated by Halley Von Dross

If I could give anyone advice at Carroll, it would be, "Be open." By that I mean… when I decided to go to Carroll as a senior in high school, I thought, "Yeah, I want to be a physical therapist. I want to do these things.." Nowhere in my right mind would I have ever thought that I would be pursuing my master's degree in psychology. I also would have never thought that I would have been someone who would be in a sorority, let alone have leadership positions, or join Student Senate.

Before going into a sorority, I think I had the impression that Greek life is all about drinking or being picture perfect or whatever you see in the movies. And I was like, "I'm not interested in that." I think when I first went, it was an ice cream social. Because I was a freshman, I went for the free ice cream. And then I met, I think, the president of Alpha Xi Delta, and she was just so easygoing, so funny, so down to earth. Not to be judgmental, but I didn't think this would be the type of person who would be in a sorority… And during the recruitment process, everyone says things like, "You're going to find your home!" and "You'll find your sisters." And I thought, "I'm not buying into any of that baloney…" Well, I was wrong. A lot of my closest friends are from my sorority, but we are also still very different. We all had different majors. Different interests. Different paths. So it was nice touching base, always having a group to turn to. And while some of them are my closest friends, some of them weren't, but that also kind of made the experience that much better because it really pushed me to be a leader in a place where I didn't think that I would be. I gained a lot of confidence. Again, I didn't expect it, but I think it really made me grow into a better person. Yes, there's a bunch of girls, so there was a lot of drama, but I learned "OK, I can be a patient individual. I can move forward with this, and not let everyone else bring me down." So there was a kind of social learning skill to it.

For my CCE, I travelled to India, and there were a couple days where they said, "Go do your own thing. Explore the city. Be back by then." I remember specifically we were trying to get to this market. Trying to find our way through the city, and obviously, there is definitely a language barrier. We'd ask to go someplace. Or a rickshaw would bring us somewhere, and we'd be like, "I don't know where we are, how are we going to get back?" That kind of thing. We got lost for a very long time. But we got to meet a bunch of different people [because] we did find some stores and everyone was like, "Come on. Drink chai with us." So we drank chai with random store owners, and then they would bring their entire families out and introduce them to us… Getting lost with friends was, I think, my favorite memory.

…This being open to whatever opportunities come–just go with it! Yes, you might have a plan, but be open to knowing that it's going to change, that it's OK if it changes; it doesn't mean your life's over… Whoever you're going to be… you're going to find that person; it's going to happen.

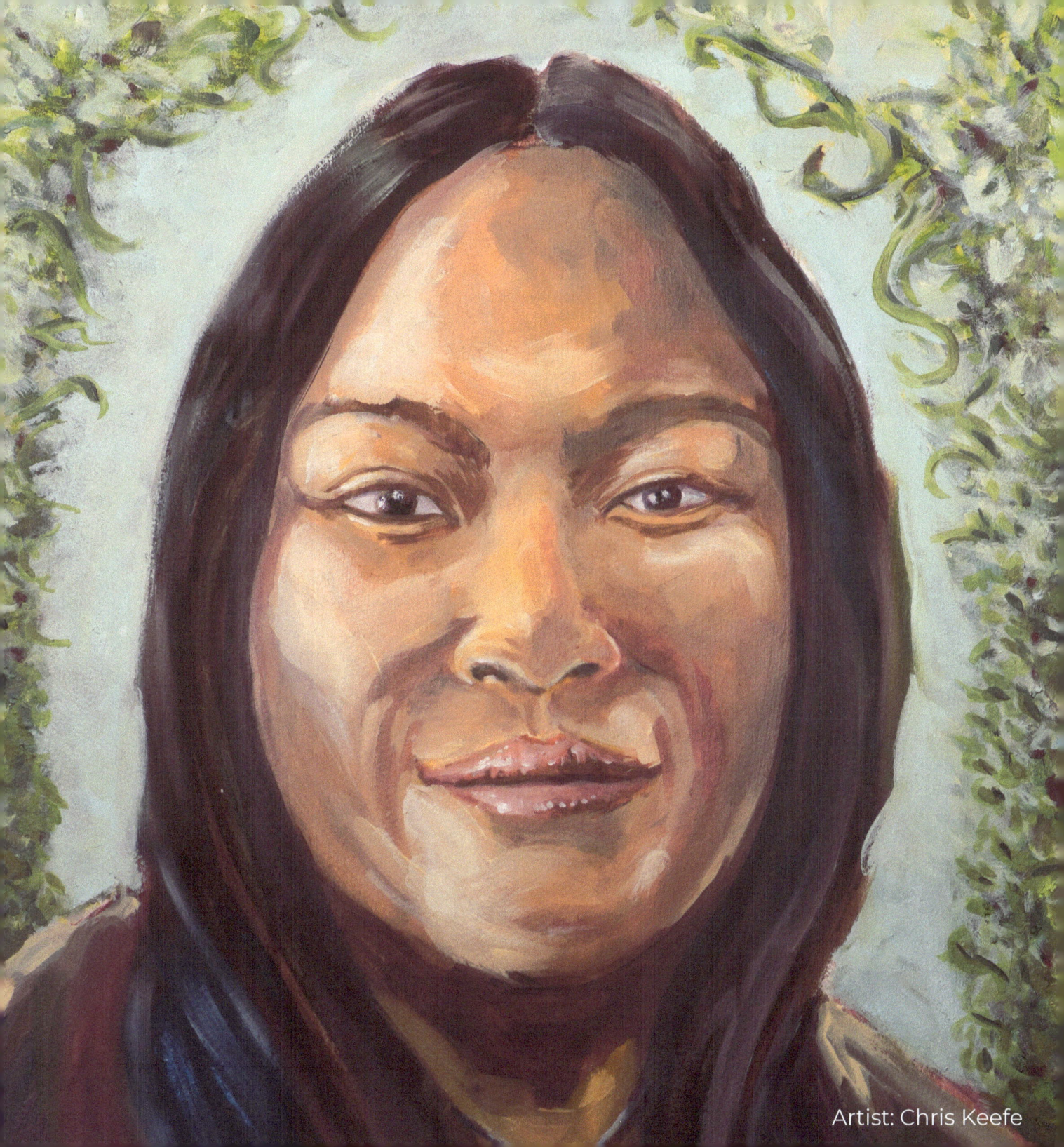

Artist: Chris Keefe

Isabella Ruggiero

Build each other up

Interviewed by Emma Kern, nominated by Rachel Verhoef

The biggest lesson for me has been don't have expectations. In high school, I had this picture of myself, like who I wanted to be, what I wanted to do, and kind of had these things planned out, and I just kind of assumed that they would happen. I thought I was going to get several awards in high school, and then didn't win them. Or coming to Carroll—I thought I was going to go to this school in New York and that didn't happen. Or my relationship with my boyfriend—sophomore year of high school, we had been friends, and I thought, "I'm going to date this guy. I'm going to date for a week so I can get it out of my system; it's not going anywhere." We'll be dating for five years in April. Or studying abroad. I always said I was going to go to Italy. I'm fifty percent Italian; I have family in Italy. But no, I did not go to Italy; I studied in Vienna, Austria, which was fantastic. It was great. But again, I had this plan for myself, and that totally got washed away.

I think some people of our generation are raised to think, "You have to be a doctor. You have to be a lawyer." You know, you have to be to be super successful. That was never my parents' strategy. Senior year of high school, my mom sat me and my brother down and asked us to share this piece of cake. We were like, "Why are we having cake?" She told us that we had a brother we'd never known about. She had given him up for adoption. He had actually written my mom a letter trying to find her. So now I have a half-brother in my life and sister-in-law and two nephews. That was a big perspective change; I thought I had this perfect, normal nuclear family, and I now didn't have that...

I don't know if we will ever be siblings in the way that society thinks that siblings should be. We have a lot of different experiences, and it's really hard to create this connection with someone who comes into your life after twenty-eight years. I mean, you wouldn't force a friendship that didn't work, but with family, we do that, right? We try and extend the arm... I'm not trying to say that our relationship is... *bad* necessarily. I just think a lot of people think it should be perfect, and it's not. American society kind of creates this idea that if you're family, we love you no matter what, right? And again, this image, these expectations of having this perfect family or whatever.

My mom has also taught me to be honest with myself. For a while, I wanted to be a teacher. I thought I was going to be an English teacher, and she would just keep asking me, "Well, do you think you could deal with this type of kid? Do you think you could do it?" Asking me those difficult questions is one thing that she's never... shied away from.

My main thing is I want people to continue to build each other up instead of breaking each other down. In adulthood, we feel the need to kind of... *combat* each other and win over other people. And I think that eventually, there's a point where people realize that they have to work together in order to get things done. I hope people do that—continue building toward a broader vision instead of just personal success. Even in this country, that's definitely one thing that I have concerns about; I think a lot of people also have concerns about that.

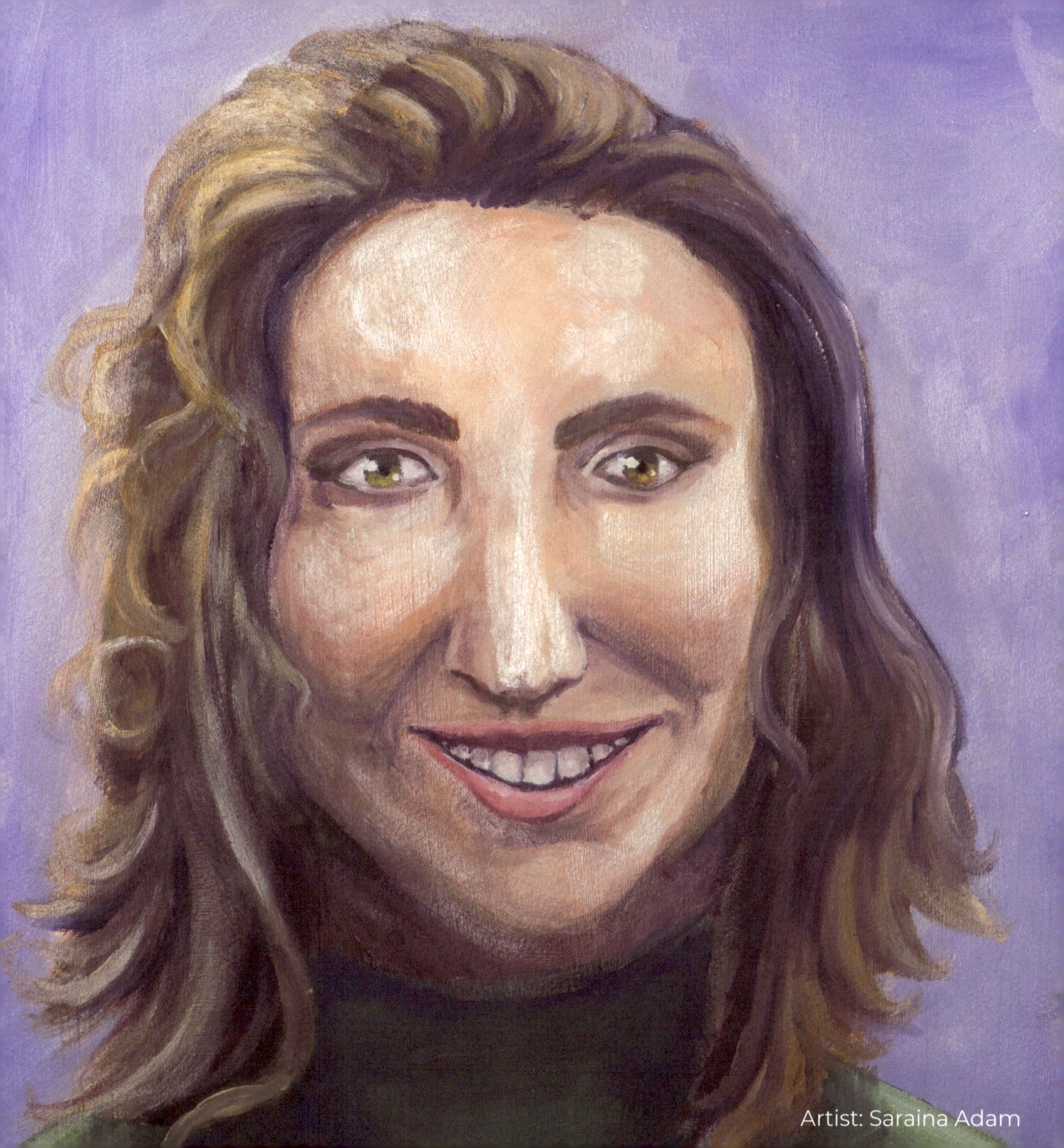

Artist: Saraina Adam

Tuna (Rosalie) Wallace

No one is better than anybody else   *Interviewed by Casaundra Johnson, nominated by Joanne Passaro*

My name? Well, I reminded my grandparents in Chicago of a little girl nicknamed Tuna. They never actually called me that, but it caught on with my other grandparents from northern Wisconsin. They all call me Tuna. My real name is Rosalie, which I don't go by at all. My brother, from the time I was born—I'm the youngest of three children—always called me Tuna, and my sister always called me Lee. I don't even like tuna fish; I actually can't stand it. It was just a comment in passing by my grandparents.

We were raised going to church. I learned a lot about God and Jesus that I believe in. Right now, I go to church, but I'm not a strong church person as far as going to women's groups or all of this other stuff. That's always been very important to me is my faith. I think just going to church, I learned some values that way and just common-sense stuff. You do something stupid and your parents go, "What the heck did you do that for?" You learn you meet people in all aspects of life, and hopefully, each one of them can teach you something.

When I started at Carroll, I was a night cook, and I worked with Jovita Garcia; she taught me so much! . Actually, going back a couple years when I worked at this little greasy spoon up North, that woman taught me how to make some basic things like chicken noodle soup and chicken dumpling soup. I loved making soups. That's what I'm famous for around here. When you have fresh chicken dumpling soup on, I have to make it for them, but normally we run a frozen soup. I don't prepare too much anymore. Not in the kitchen, because I've been a kitchen supervisor, so I cook lunches. I cook usually a Saturday brunch, and if someone calls in sick, then I'm a fill-in cook. But when I worked here with Joni, she taught me how to do catering trays. She taught me how to take a top round and cut it into sirloin steaks. She influenced me greatly. She is, I think, the best cook in Waukesha. She would still be working here if she didn't have some health concerns. She was by far, like I said, the best cook I've ever worked with.

I learned the importance of the need to work with your staff and hopefully train them to be a family rather than catty. You know what they always say about women in a kitchen. My job relies on my staff. I can't do the job if my staff doesn't provide me with the insight I need as far as how much I need to order. I do a lot of tracking. I have paperwork that they fill out as far as, "I use this much meat. I made this many kinds of that." If I didn't have that it wouldn't run smooth, and it's just trying to get people to take responsibility for the position that they're holding. If someone is held accountable, they're more likely to give you correct insight. It's making everyone feel important because my dishwashers are just as important as my cooks. No one is better than anybody in that kitchen.

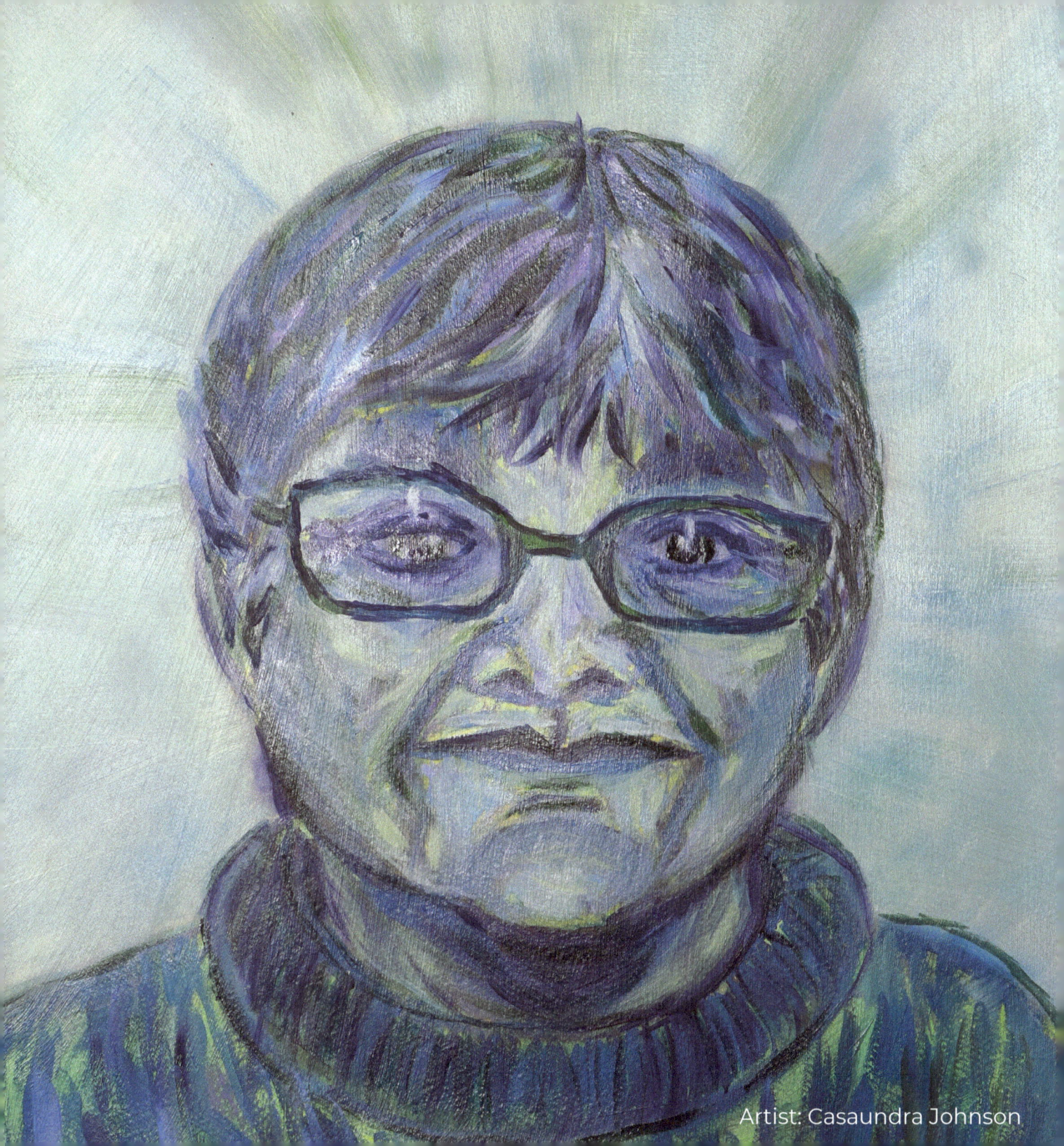

Artist: Casaundra Johnson

Maureen Klopp

Health as a human right

Interviewed by David Meza & Liz Casciato, nominated anonymously

I studied public health and had an internship with the Environmental Protection Agency. And so I got to do some work with a community in Pennsylvania that was looking at lead and water and other public health problems they have. We were just helping them gather all their data and understand where their problems were, what environmental things were causing the problems in their community. I made a whole plan, not to address the problems but understand them from a public health point of view, and then I gave them my research. They're presenting it to the community, seeing what the community thinks, and getting the community's involvement.

That's also why I want to work for the government. When I say that, a lot of people kind of go "Uhh, woahh!" But that's my goal; I just really like diseases. At a federal, state, or county health department, you're doing surveillance to see if there's any new viruses or outbreaks of viruses, like malaria, dengue, yellow fever… With some experience, I could be going abroad to see why outbreaks are happening, what we can do, how to stop spreading it…. Climate change is a huge topic whenever we talk about any type of disease because of how all the weather is shifting, and how that shifts where animals are going, and shifts diseases to new places. It's never been seen before… And I find it very interesting, so lot of my free time, I spend looking at vaccines, looking up different countries, how they're doing, and what they're doing.

My interest in public health came from Carroll. My adviser encouraged me to find out what I liked in public health. And then another professor, she really got me interested in global health….There are so many places where, if they get basic needs filled or some simple resources, they can have a better quality of life and a longer life. That inspired me to go for my master's degree. I also took a postcolonial literature class at Carroll that definitely… I didn't really want to take the class, but my friend recommended it to me, and it was really… a public health class too—analyzing literature and groups being marginalized in literature. Their stories and what happened to them, it was really an eye-opening class.

…The pandemic made me realize how important politics is… I knew politics was important, but not how much politics can actually do… the Affordable Care Act really did help so many people; taking parts of that away, which Trump was planning on doing, really would have hurt how much we've accomplished healthwise… I view health as a human right; it's something that you shouldn't have to be making a certain income to get… You should always deserve the best care that you have to live the longest life that you can… That's another reason I want to go into public health; I want to help guide change.

A large part of public health is getting knowledge into communities through community interventions and community activism. For example, we know racial inequalities lead to really bad, horrible health outcomes… As a public health person, you hate to see that just because you're born with a certain skin color, you have a ten-year shorter life expectancy than someone born with a different skin color. It shouldn't matter what color you are born… Everyone should have the same life expectancy when they're first born, no matter what.

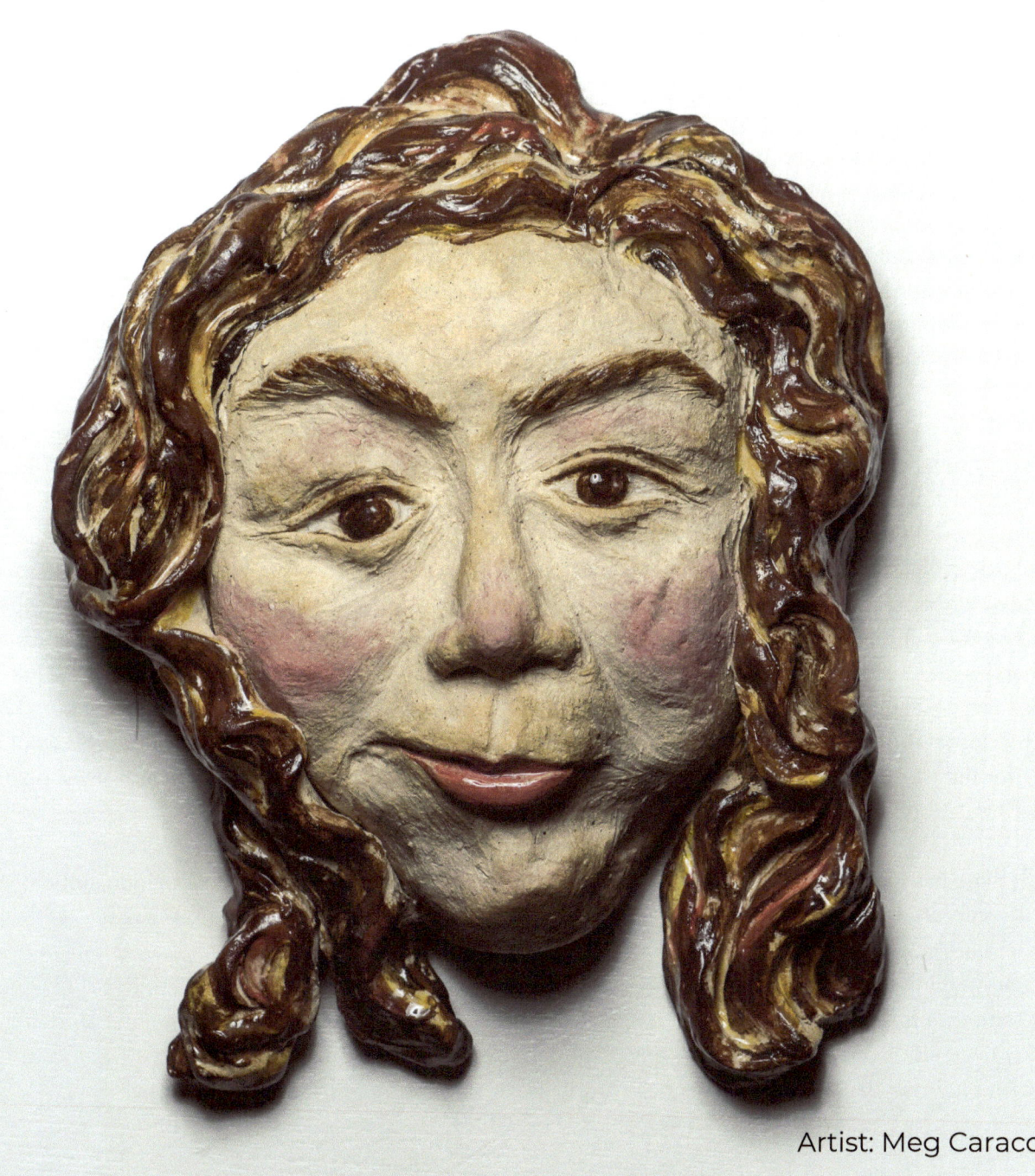

Artist: Meg Caracci

Brandon Koster
Back at the beginning

Interviewed by Madeleine Buchta, nominated by Sara Meyer

I grew up about twenty minutes from Carroll, in Muskego. I was born in Milwaukee and moved right before kindergarten. My parents thought it would be a safer environment to bring up a six year old. I learned later that our neighbor was robbed and then our neighbor on the other side. So my parents decided to find someplace new. That landed me a stone's throw away from Carroll.

I definitely wish I could redo my first two years at Carroll. As a commuter, my day consisted of four classes back to back-to-back-to-back so I could get home and play those damn video games. I was one of those people who got through the important parts of the day just to get home and play six hours of video games. It sucked away my life. Looking back, it was fun but I definitely wish I'd used my time differently…

I was a history major before Professor Zager cornered me after taking his Theater 101 class. At that point, the theater program here was hurting for male talent. So I got roped into a show and then couldn't leave. The first theater production I was in was *Imaginary Invalid* by Moliere. It was a big leap for me, going from the library nerd who did nothing but read his books and play video games to… Well, all of a sudden I'm on campus at nine o'clock at night, rehearsing for this ridiculous show, having to wear very, *very* strange costumes. I wasn't very knowledgeable about theater. It was the first time I got to see what a rehearsal process was like, what it was like working under a director, what was expected of you. I definitely learned more in that month and a half of rehearsals than I did in that semester-long class. It's theater. You have to actively learn. You can't just read in a book. I remember thinking, "I can't believe I'm doing this!" Now, several years in the future, it's where I met all of my closest friends; it's where I made all of my strongest connections. It's just an experience I wouldn't change for the world. I started Carroll with a passion for history and ended with a passion for history, politics, and the theater arts.

Another thing I've learned from ten years in higher education is that it's definitely where I belong, not only because it's comfortable and familiar to me. I have that urge to help the people around me—to really guide and advise and assist, and to teach. Not only my peers, but also the students, as well as the scared families looking at Carroll thinking, "How am I going to afford this for my son?" Or the girl that's trying to decide between twelve schools. I feel I have a pretty unique upbringing in that I went from a shut-out commuter student to a really involved student, and from a small, private undergraduate institution to experiencing life at a "Big Ten" school. And now I'm back at the beginning, back where it started at Carroll. I feel I have a lot to give…

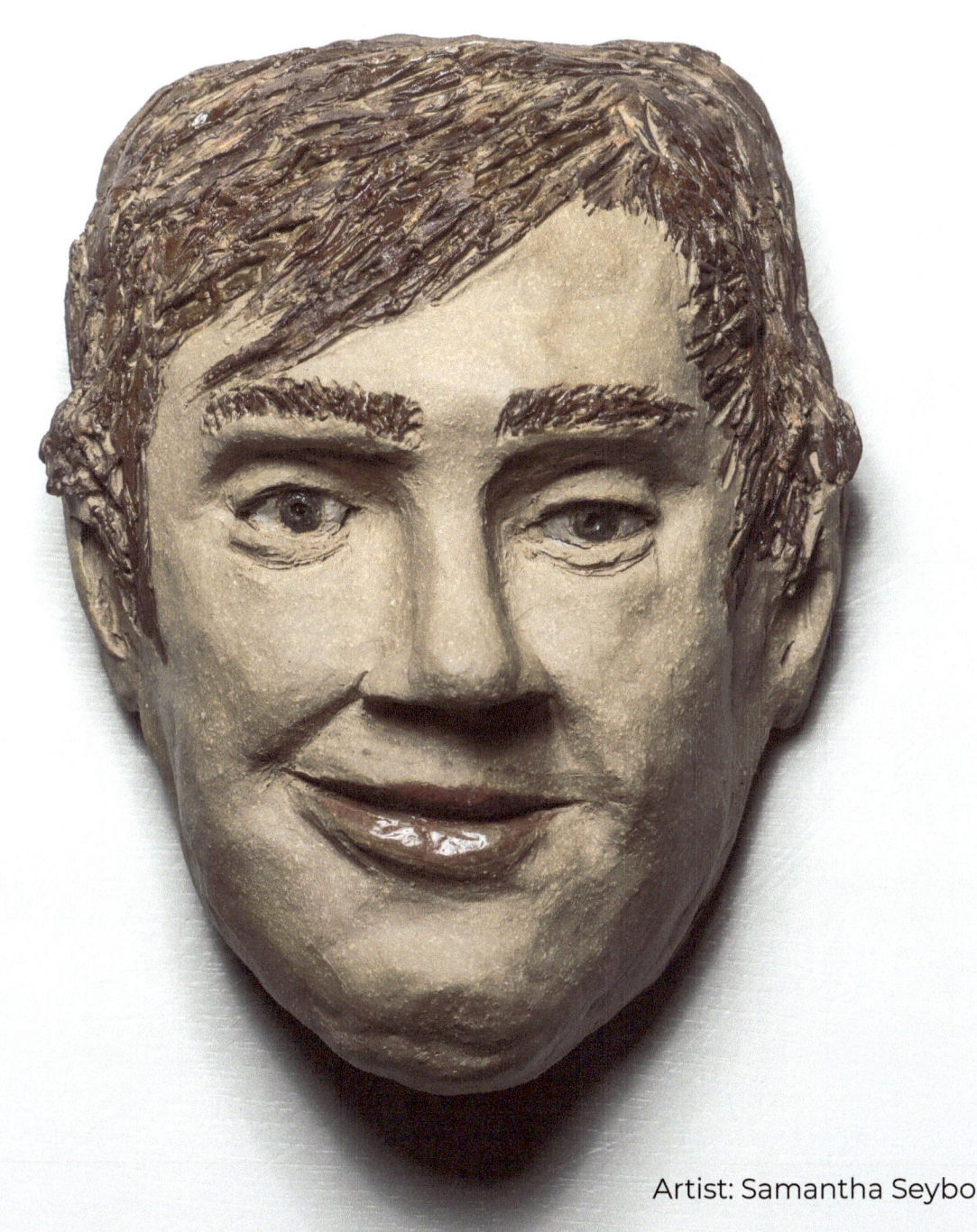

Artist: Samantha Seybold

Scott Celsor

If you don't grow...

Interviewed by Alexandria Dollhopf and Skylar Harmsen, nominated by Jessica Mueller

I went to college at a small fundamentalist school. They emphasize combining Biblical teachings with science... taking a Biblical focus and incorporating it into all areas, even my majors: economics and management. I thought it might be good to have an accounting minor. By senior year, I was sick of business; I realized I wanted to something different [and] I'd taken up a third major in ministry. So I graduated with 178 credit hours—3 majors and a minor. So now, I tell my students today in class, "I know your interests are going to change. You don't quite know who you are. That's fine. That's the way it should be, but do us all a favor and change your major! Don't just keep adding them and keeping the old ones!" Education is important, but... it's not wise to focus on that to the point you don't do anything else. I had 178 credit hours... but I didn't do anything else!

...Eventually I enrolled in graduate school in philosophy—for which I was totally not prepared! ...I'd had only one philosophy course as an undergrad, so when I studied it at the graduate level, I was thoroughly unprepared. It was a difficult two years, but it might have been the most important two years of my life... So basically, those other two [undergrad] majors and that minor... served no purpose in my life. Those 40 hours, that itty bitty major, that's the one I focused my life around. It's just strange how life does that to people...

...I'm a Christian theologian... What that means is that I present a wide variety of views on how to read the Bible. You can read it from an evangelical standpoint, a fundamentalist, a liberal protestant, or a Catholic perspective. I present all these different positions, which makes it easier for students to understand because it relates to [whatever] they grew up with. But then I challenge them: "Look at these other positions! You're in college! It's time to take what you were taught as a child and reflect on it. Do I think this is right, or do I see problems with it? That's what you need to do at this point.... Otherwise, if you don't grow... what good is that? It's not you."

My own faith has very much evolved... I've come to the appreciation that while it's important to understand the Church's position and what Scripture has to say, there's a very real component of culture adding things to the scriptures... There are different religious cultures; they each have a particular way of reading the Bible. If you're in a particular culture, that way of reading looks obvious. If you're in another, it doesn't look to be quite so obvious. From my standpoint, it's fairly clear: culture contributes to your reading of the Bible, your understanding of faith, of Christian ethics.... and it will continue to evolve.

There's more of an emphasis today on teaching world religions... and of course 9/11 accelerated that... Thirty years ago... there was still an emphasis on a search for Truth. I don't see that emphasis today. Religion is more confined to a point of opinion, there's no real Truth to it anymore. That makes it much more difficult to teach religion, that shift from a modern to a postmodern mindset... [And] that did challenge my childhood faith, [but] I had to go through what I did to get where I am now.

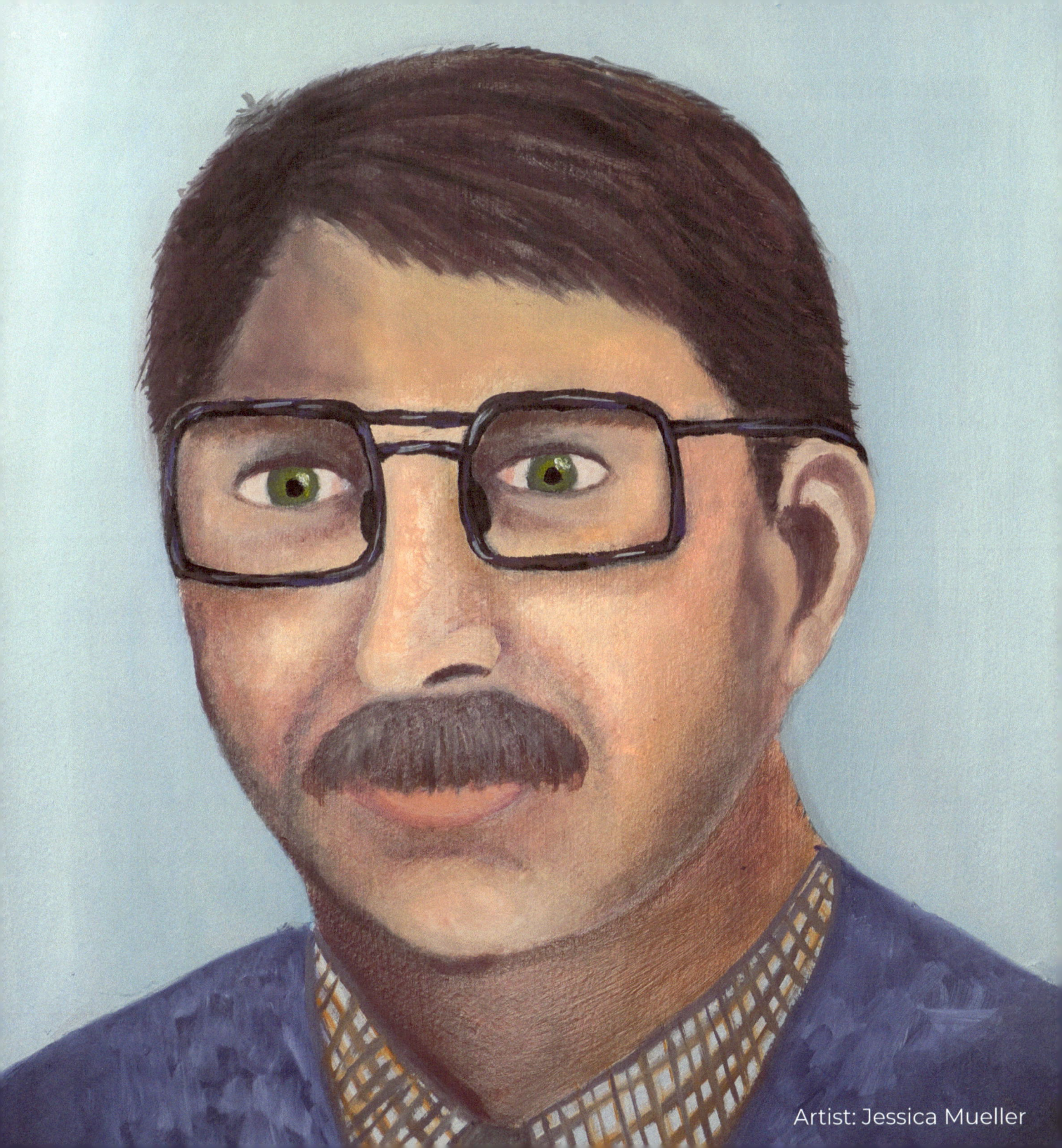

Artist: Jessica Mueller

David Simpson
Intellectually curious

Interviewed by Abbi Hess, nominated by Carole Stein

My values are a function of my family, and my family allowed me to be intellectually curious. Where most children might be subscribing to a children's magazine, I read the *Saturday Review of Literature*. Some children like to make forts; I liked to have an office. Downstairs in the basement, I had my own office, and my dad would bring back all these little pocket books that have maps on them and things of that sort.

I was the valedictorian of my high school. I went from high school, as a National Merit Scholar, to Oberlin College in Ohio. Oberlin was very formative for me. I went there really with no political values, no interaction with the opposite sex. I found myself at a school where the freshman class had thirty National Merit Scholars. It was very humbling.

[I switched] from an education major to a psychology major, in part because I had to take two semesters of psychology. In the first semester, [we dealt] with primarily physiological and sensation reception; the second semester was more on social psychology, and that excited me quite a bit. My advisor got me very interested in psychological testing. Another professor, Ralph Turner—a psychology professor—became my friend, mentor, advisor. He was the first faculty member I had an opportunity to call by his first name. He was a really good teacher. He was intellectually curious. His office was just full of books, and his specialty was social psychology. So I became very interested in society.

I loved learning. I really wanted to go on. There was more I wanted to learn, but I'd learned enough from Oberlin. I walked around; I knew every building. I wasn't that good a student, but I learned so much from my fellow students. I learned so much about social justice issues, different ways of teaching. I wanted to go on.

I applied to six schools: Harvard, Madison, Michigan State, Northwestern, University of Chicago, and Ohio State. Ralph, my advisor, had graduated from Ohio State, and I heard they were really good in attitudinal and measurement things. I got accepted to Ohio State and was offered tons of money. More importantly, I kept getting wonderful correspondence from a professor there, Tom Hoster. I was blessed with who I got as an advisor. Tom was my advisor for seven years. He was kind, and he was patient with somebody who didn't have the research skills that everyone else did. One hundred applications, and only five of us were accepted. Four of them already had two or three publications in prestigious journals, but it was quite apparent that I was not destined to become the high-powered Ohio State researchers my classmates became.

I was destined to go into teaching somewhere down the road, but with a really strong foundation in research. Tom put in my mailbox a job application that was already six months old, for a place called Carroll College. I got invited for an interview on December 11th, 1977, a two-day interview. All these pieces kind of fell together, and a week after the interview, I was offered a job. This is my forty-first year at Carroll, [and] that's how I got here.

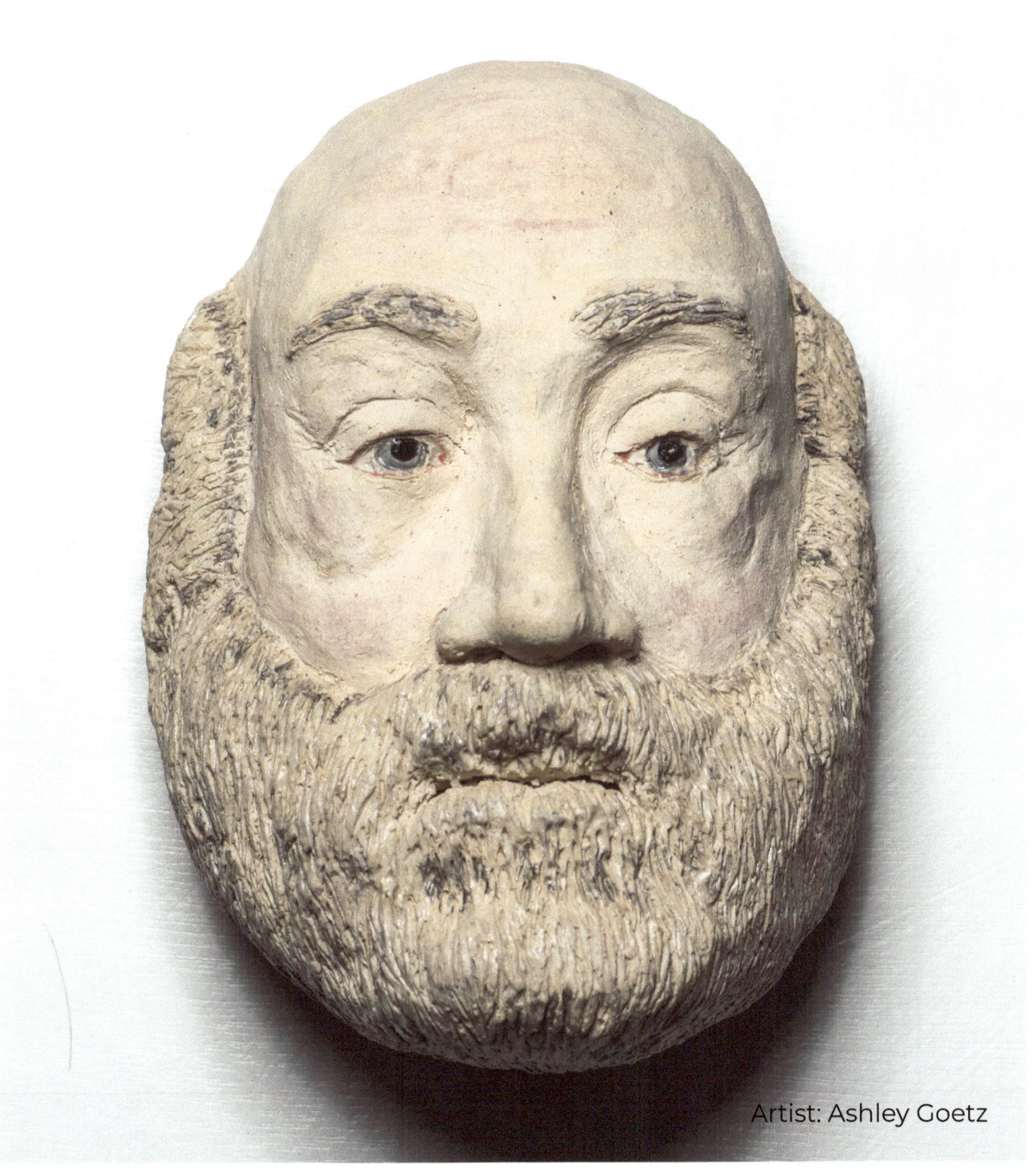

Artist: Ashley Goetz

Bethany Kelly
What hope looks like

Interviewed by Claudia Splice, nominated anonymously

What brought me to Carroll was the dual certification program for elementary and special education because it's only at [a few] schools and I wanted to do both. I'm very passionate about rights for people who have disabilities and about education within that realm, too. Making sure every child, no matter where they come from or what abilities they have, gets a quality education, and an education that fits their needs, even if it's not like the way other students learn. It's just really important to base education towards each specific child. And that's one of the reasons I'm going into the field...

I want to ensure that each child gets through the year learning something really memorable because my brother went through the school system, and it didn't work super well for him. My brother has an intellectual disability [and] functions at the level of a three- or four-year-old. He's 22 years old... He's taught me to have patience with people and to understand that people... might not have the same skills as we have, but they're still people, and they should be valued as they are. And he's really taught me just how important loving people is because it's sometimes... I love him to death. Obviously. But it can be difficult. Especially when he's having a tantrum in a store; at the age of 22, he can be a little scary for other people. That's another reason for my whole special needs rights thing. I don't want that to be scary for people because it's not. In that case, it's just that he was triggered...

I know I want to work with younger kids, but I don't know if I want to do general education—kindergarten or first grade—or special education. This whole year, I've been working at Randall STEM (Science Technology Engineering and Mathematics) Academy, where I'm in a combined kindergarten and first grade classroom. One student I work with has an IEP (Individualized Educational Plan). And just working with him, that one-on-one exposure, has been really beneficial for me. Whenever I work with kids, they give me hope in the smallest ways. Just their ability to find the funniest things—not actually funny, but the most random things—hilarious. Just the innocence they bring, and their curiosity, that gives me hope.

For kids with special needs, hope looks like each child having an individualized learning plan for themselves. No matter what needs they have. And that's easily obtainable for each individual student. For example, one student reads really fast, but might not get the comprehension, but then another student might. I just feel like if each student has an individualized plan and support for themselves, then they can exceed at a far higher caliber than they would [if they learned] about what everyone else is learning about because everyone learns in a different way. My biggest worry would just be people seeing people for their disabilities, rather than for the person that they are underneath the disabilities. A person isn't just their disability; they're an actual person.

I want to be that teacher that kids remember: "Oh yeah, this teacher. She's the one who gave me hope and made me think I was a good learner." I just want to be that favorite teacher; the one kids remember and who impacts their lives.

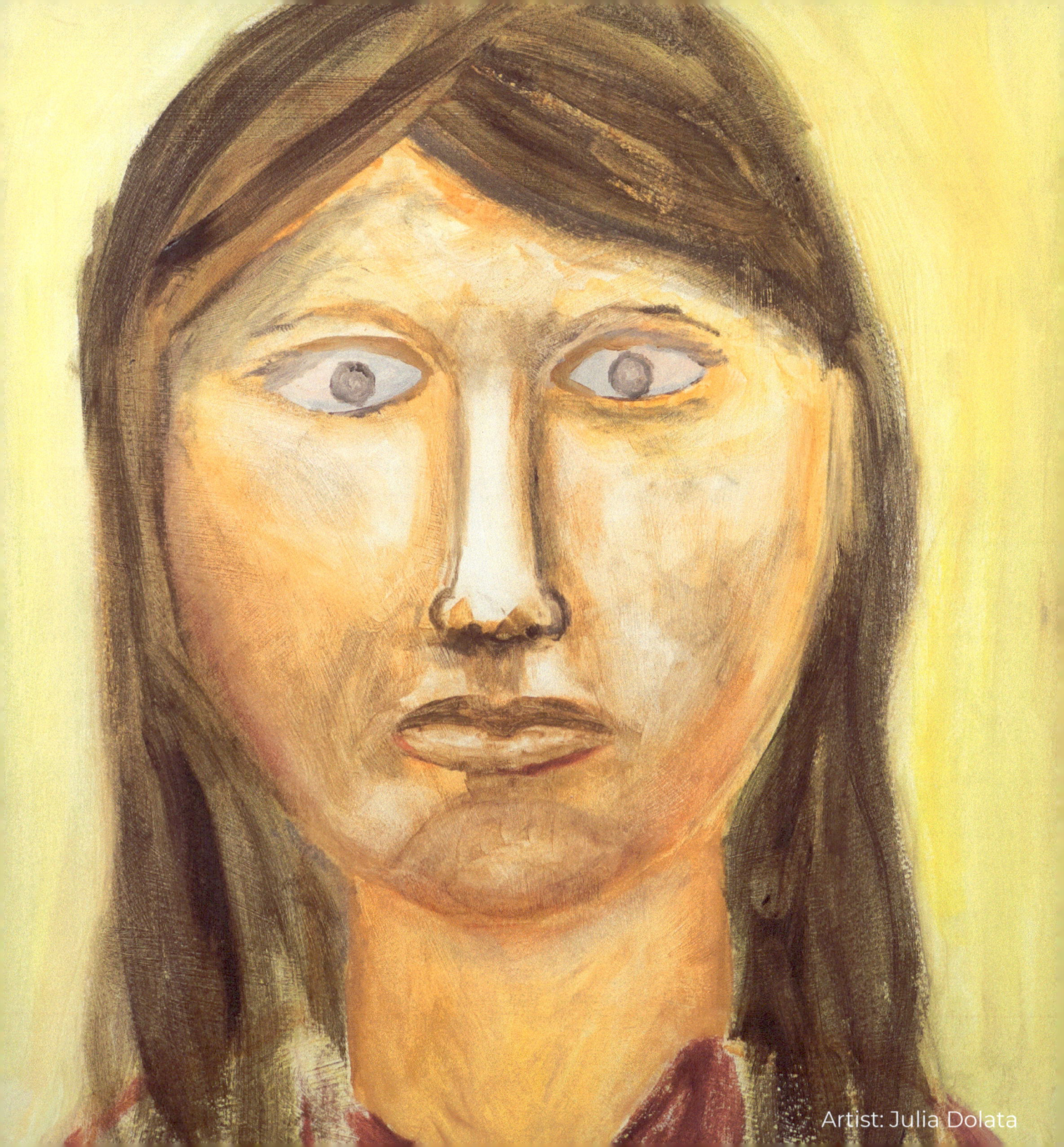

Artist: Julia Dolata

Deeper (in)sights: Voices of Carroll at 172

Carroll University's 2017-18 *(in)sight* project provided an interdisciplinary lens through which to explore the values and visions of students, staff, and faculty. While campus and community artists worked in paint, pastels, or clay, other students captured insights through qualitative, life-history-style interviews.[1] These 30-60 minute interviews reveal diverse interests and experiences, but they also share a tendency to focus on four kinds of relationships: familial (biological and chosen), "taking," romantic, and aromantic.

Sociologists explain that these types of relationships enhance individuals' sense of "mattering," i.e. of feeling "significant and important to other people."[2] Carroll aims to nurture this sense of mattering by fostering close-knit communities and personal development. Faculty, staff, and students alike seem to recognize the value of being seen. A perception of mattering—that one's individual growth and insights are valued—generates the confidence and motivation to influence collective behaviors and norms.[3] This is important, because the *(in)sight* project used a nomination-based selection process. Models were chosen (and knew they were chosen) because another member of the campus community perceives them as mattering here and now. Participants have social capital within the Carroll community, and the interviews show that they used this capital—this publicly-recognized mattering—to articulate the powerful lessons of close, private relationships.

Familial Relationships

Not surprisingly, family ties create a sense of "mattering." Individuals who feel secure in familial relationships tend to have better self-esteem and are less likely to think about suicide. Out of the eighteen people who were asked explicitly, "Who is the most important or influential person in your life?" sixteen identified a family member, usually because they modelled life values. Moms were mentioned the most. For example, Carl Ervin talked about how his mom taught him to put God first, then family. This becomes even more evident in his interview when he described his belonging to his church, when he really grasped her teaching that "your purpose in life is more than just you."[4] Jessica Perez, a student at Carroll University, explains how her mom promotes a sense of mattering: "She's always been there for me. Every time I am having a hard day or time, I go to her and immediately I feel better. Even if she doesn't say anything back. Just [being able to tell] her what I'm feeling."[5]

---

1 History majors, led by Dr. Kimberly A. Redding, developed interview guidelines. Interviews were conducted by students in select Communication, Composition and History courses. On Saskia de Rooy, see her website: "Art for Life."
2 Gordon Flett et al., "Mattering and Psychological Well-being in College and University Students: Review and Recommendations for Campus-Based Initiatives," *International Journal of Mental Health and Addiction* 17, no.3 (2019): 667.
3 George Loewenstein et al., "On Mattering Map," in *Understanding Choice, Explaining Behavior: Essays in Honour of Ole-Jorgen Skog,* ed. Jon Elster et al. (Oslo: Oslo Academic Press, 2006), 154, 159; Gregory C. Elliott, *Family Matters: The Importance of Mattering to Family in Adolescence* (Wiley-Blackwell, 2009), 2.
4 Carl Ervin, "A better future today," interview by Amanda Elkins and Kayla Geissberger, April 2018.
5 Jessica Perez, "Everything happens for a reason," interview by Elaine Yarger, April 2018.

Hannah Prosser mentions only two specific people in herentire interview. One is her mom, who signed her up for dance lessons when she was three years old. Eventually, Hannah's mom opened a dance studio in their hometown of Beaver Dam to spare them both the 80-minute round trip to lessons in Fond Du Lac; she now makes a living running multiple dance studios. The way Hannah talks about her mom shows her recognition of these actions as a demonstration of mattering.

Numerous participants describe grandmothers as important maternal figures, which is interesting because it challenges American societal norms that stress the nuclear family more than multi-generational support networks. For example, Dawn Scott talks about her grandmother the way others talk about their mothers:

> I lived with her [full-time from] when I was 15 and just [felt] an overwhelming sense of belonging. She would never let us down. She was always there for you. You know, she knew all of the little things, you know that were important… core of our family.[6]

Scott moved in with her grandparents to gain more work and social opportunities. She found, along with that, a greater sense of mattering.

While more than 90% of interviewees mention their mothers, only about two-thirds talk about their fathers.[7] Maggie Treants is one of few who says their father is the most important figure in life:

> He takes care of our family and my grandma… all the stuff he's done in his life, he just keeps pushing. I have never met somebody with drive like that. Every time I feel like something is the end of the world for me—a really bad situation—I think, 'Ok, he got through.'[8]

Less surprisingly, spouses and children are also talked about—children more than spouses. Greg Gabrielsen brings them up within the first 35 seconds of conversation:

> I'm married, and I have two kids. I enjoy my children, and they are quite time consuming; that's my... I don't have a whole lot of time for interesting things because I've got a toddler. My daughter's almost three and my son's almost one, so they eat up most of the minutes of my day that I am not actively here.

---

6 Dawn Scott, "Bring me your student," interview by Elaine Yarger, April 2018.
7 This count does not include interviews that only mention fathers in collective phrases like "mom and dad."
8 Maggie Treants, "Get past your fear," interview by Alyssa Polewaczyk and Desirae Dunn, April 2018.

Ten minutes later, Gabrielsen mentions his children a second time, describing their births as the happiest moments in his life. Parenting promotes his sense of mattering: "Everything still goes back to my kids and getting focused on that."[9] Dawn Scott mentions her kids as a source of both worry and hope, suggesting that mattering may not be linked to control or positivity. Still, she too recognizes relationships with her children as essential sources of purpose and identity, i.e. of mattering.[10]

"Taking" Relationships

Another category of relationships involves non-familial, asymmetrical circumstances in which interviewees recognized they have taken or drawn support from people in authority—advisors, professors, employers, etc. Carroll staff members most often bring up what I call "taking" relationships. Financial aid counselor and alumnus Brandon Koster includes two professors this way:

> I remember looking at Dr. Hendrix, hearing him talk [and] thinking to myself, 'Damn, I want to do that someday. I want to teach, be in a university setting...' He was the foundation of my [goal to work as a] higher education instructor.[11]

Soon after, Koster took a theater course taught by Professor James Zager. As an introvert and commuter student, Koster says he lacked that "college experience" until Zager helped him become more outgoing and involved.

This type of student-teacher bond is also important to David Simpson, a retired faculty member whose narrative is full of stories about his educational past. He describes at length the undergrad professor who sparked his interest in social psychology. Dr. Ralph Turner "became my friend, mentor, advisor. He was the first faculty member I called by their first name." Turner encouraged Simpson to take on challenges such as writing his first book. Simpson also notes the giving nature of a graduate school professor: "He was just bending over backwards. 'David, here is a list of all my publications. Call me anytime.'" [12] The professor's willingness to work with Simpson, who felt underprepared for grad school, created a deep bond. Simpson worked under Hoster for seven years, even following him to Norway at one point. He cites this giving researcher for helping him identify and pursue his own passion: teaching.

9 Greg Gabrielsen, "A huge gap," interview by Mia Pham, April 2018.
10 Kenneth Barish, "We Are Always Essential," in *Parenting: Contemporary Clinical Perspectives, ed. Stephen Tuber* (Lanham: Rowman and Littlefield, 2016), 62.
11 Brandon Koster, "Back at the Beginning," interviewed by Madeleine Buchta, April 2018.
12 Dr. David Simpson, "Intellectually curious," interviewed by Abbi Hess, April 2018.

Clearly, asymmetrical relationships can create a heightened sense of mattering. Yet they are not evident in current students' interviews. A few mention professors or supervisors in passing, but their comments lack the richness shown by Koster, Simpson, and others, even though institutional literature promotes the student-teacher relationships that are possible due to Carroll's small class sizes. Perhaps these asymmetrical relationships just stand out more in retrospect, or maybe current students are simply not yet aware how their instructors matter outside the classroom.[13]

Romantic Relationships

Romantic relationships seem even more influential, regardless of age, and were described as providing emotional support, companionship, and even vocational guidance. Wade Chamberlin, for example, described his girlfriend as prompting an "aha" realization during a period of doubt about his major field of study:

> My girlfriend was saying, "You know, you're really good at that stuff, I've seen you mess around with it. You know what you're doing; why don't you just try it?" And then I realized that the classes that I would have been to or that I was taking or would have taken after I switched are not.[14]

Similarly, student Amanda Collette recalls her boyfriend's reaction to her indecisiveness: "He said to stop saying things and just to start doing them."[15]

Student participant Thitikan Thianjan immigrated to Wisconsin from Thailand in 2012. She credits her boyfriend for being there to support her and helping her adjust to American life. Thianjan stated, "He's gonna be there to support me. So it just makes me feel a little bit confident about myself."[16]

In college, a major form of mattering is seen in perceptions of romantic relationships; positive romance creates a high sense of mattering. This helps explain why students brought up their partners. As emerging adults, they are at the stage of human development where they are able to have long-term, committed relationships.[17] These romantic relationships among emerging adults symbolize "emotional autonomy" and furthers the shift towards total independence.[18] As shown, participants describe their romantic relationships in this way.

---

13 Patricia K. Kerig et al., "The Transition from Adolescence to Adulthood," in *Adolescence and Beyond*, ed. Kerig et al, (New York: Oxford University Press, 2012), 5-6.
14 Wade Chamberlin, "Seeing yourself evolve," interviewed by Elizabeth Boziel, April 2018.
15 Amanda Collette, "A bridge," interviewed by Emily Poffinbarger, April 2018.
16 Thitikan Thianjan "Expectations," interviewed by Corey Kowalski and Cassidy Neefe, April 2018.
17 Kerig et al., "Transition," 5-6.
18 Patricia K. Kerig et al.,, "Friendships and Intimate Relationships," in *Adolescence and Beyond*, ed. Kerig et al, (New York: Oxford University Press, 2012), 85.

Aromantic Relationships

This category includes peers: roommates, non-marital romantic partners, and a variety of aromantic relationships. Current students seem far more likely than faculty or staff to bring up peer relationships, likely because students are grouped by age through their schooling. On campus, these connections evolve quickly; a stranger can become a roommate, and then a confidante. From the outside, peer relationships often blur into a vast network of interpersonal associations. Mattering within that network boosts opportunities for formative experiences outside the classroom and is a critical feature of American higher education.

Some studies suggest that college roommates help students learn to be more psychologically aware of unappealing differences.[19] However, the two students who talked at length about their roommates focused on positive attributes, perhaps because they had chosen to live together. Shelby Stephan explained:

> Two of my roommates that are in the nursing program with me, we're super close, and we do everything together all the time because we're in classes together and we go back and live together. So they're just always together, so then they kind of almost like sisters in a way now because it's been three years.[20]

Similarly, Isabelle Banke recalled her roommates' support after heart surgery:

> I lived with two nursing majors and two other pre-med majors. So like for me to be like, "Hey, can you help me take a shower? They were like, "yeah we can." You know, it was one of those things where, like, this is so nice. And I didn't feel dumb about it because everyone that I live with, it's what they want to do with their lives. And so it wasn't weird at all.[21]

It may seem obvious why students choose to mention positive roommate relationships in this quasi-public situation; they've internalized a polite midwestern norm: If you don't have anything nice to say; don't anything at all. On the other hand, "the roommate from hell" is a recognized trope in college life; the significance of less-than-ideal roommate relationships may also be something that is understood over time.

---

19 Daniel F. Chambliss et al., *How College Works* (Cambridge: Harvard University Press, 2014) 87, 94.
20 Shelby Stephan, "Open mind, open heart," interviewed by Julia Nelson, April 2018.
21 Isabelle Banke, "Invisible scars," interviewed by Katie Dobrzynski, April 2018.

Aromantic relationships also include what (in)sight participants described as friendships of circumstance. For example, Maggie Treants found solidarity in high school when she bonded with a bunch of "misfits":

> They'd say it's like the zombie survival squad because you all band together; you all have different skills and things like that. And then once the apocalypse is over, you go your separate ways. We were all kind of the misfits of people who didn't fit in. And we all had this huge… a massive social group of maybe 14 people; all of us just bonded together.

Maggie met her best friend online, and they both have similar interests even though their stories—how they got to Carroll, and where they are going—are quite different One of Maggie's happiest moments in life was meeting her best friend and going to a concert of a band that they had bonded over together for a long time.[22]

Office Manager Jocelyn Guzman relied on an aromantic, maybe even anonymous, relationship to help her get out of her comfort zone. Jocelyn notes going to a "One Tree Hill" (popular TV show) convention as a major breakthrough because she put herself in a public situation with multiple people. Meeting and bonding with another fan was a life-changing moment; she overcame her social anxiety and made connections based on shared interest.[23]

Wade Chamberlain also spoke about relationships formed by a common interest: football for Carroll. Being part of the football team helped him be a part of a social group and helped him assimilate into that college lifestyle. A lot of friends mentioned by the participants were part of a group. There are only a few examples of individual peers being talked about, perhaps because the bonds come from shared interests. When describing peers, participants talk about them as a more casual form of support and in a particular social setting, unlike romantic partners, who are credited with more active influence on participants' life paths. For college students, however, these friendship groups create a crucial feeling of belonging.[24]

---

22 Treants, interview.
23 Jocelyn Guzman, "Just keep going," interviewed by Kylie Peters, April 2018.
24 Chambliss and Takacs, "How College Works," 81.

Mattering

A constant among the interviews is the idea of belonging—mattering to something larger than one's self. In fact, few participants mention their own accomplishments. Rather, each person demonstrates that they value relationships. If there were one statement that encapsulates the spirit of these Deeper (in)sight interviews, it would be, "I belong—to my family, to my peers, to this community."

Why should we care about this project—a bunch of interviews conducted by minimally trained undergrads? Representatives of Carroll University repeatedly talk about an ideal, a vision called "The Carroll Community," but what is that? When and how do we acknowledge the psycho-social elements that actually create community? How can we understand what it means to be a part of a community we're not born into, i.e. that each one of us has chosen? How do perceptions of social mattering shape collective identity? Carroll is more than our mascot Pio Pete, our historic campus, and our traditions; we are a microcosm of a society mired in—and divided by—a collective fear of not mattering. The (in)sight project interviews remind us that engaging the interplay of mattering and sociability strengthens both individuals and communities.

—Cameron Tom with Kimberly A. Redding

References

Barish, Kenneth. "We Are Always Essential." In *Parenting: Contemporary Clinical Perspectives*, edited by Stephen Tuber, 62. Lanham: Rowman and Littlefield, 2016.

Chamblis, Daniel F., and Chris G. Tackaks. *How College Works*. Cambridge: Harvard University Press, 2014.

Elliot, Gregory C. *Family Matters: The Importance of Mattering to Family in Adolescence*. West Sussex: Wiley-Blackwell, 2009.

Flett, Gordon, Attia Khan, and Chang Su. "Mattering and Psychological Well-Being in College and University Students: Review and Recommendations for Campus-Based Initiatives." *International Journal of Mental Health & Addiction* 17, no. 3 (June 2019): 667–80. doi:10.1007/s11469-019-00073-6

Kerig, Patricia K. and Marc S. Schultz. "The Transition from Adolescence to Adulthood." In *Adolescence and Beyond*, edited by Patricia K. Kerig, Marc S. Schultz, and Stuart T. Hauser. New York: Oxford University Press, 2012.

Loewenstein, George and Karl Moene. "On Mattering Map." *Understanding Choice, Explaining Behavior: Essays in Honour of Ole-Jorgen Skog,* edited by Jon Elster et al., 153-175. Oslo: Oslo Academic Press, 2006

Institutional Identity from the Inside Out

Carroll was chartered as the Wisconsin Territory's first four-year college in 1846, one of dozens of institutions founded as the United States expanded its rule across North America. Government officials, church leaders, and homesteaders alike saw these colleges not only as part of "civilizing" the region in the wake of Indian removal, but they also saw them as a way to assure settler communities espoused Yankee (as opposed to German or Irish, for example) cultural norms and religious values. Congregationalist and Presbyterian communities had long supported New England's colleges and supported the establishment of higher education into "the West" as part of home mission evangelism efforts. That said, political and denominational conflicts often hindered attempts to charter new institutions. Carroll's founders avoided that problem by "stipulating that no religious affiliations should be required for students or faculty," meaning, as Ellen Langill notes, that "no one Protestant denomination would be preferred."[25] That said, the namesake of the college was likely Reverend Dr. Daniel Carroll, a Presbyterian pastor from New York who had served as president of Hampton-Sidney College and was a vocal advocate of the home missionary movement. Furthermore, Carroll's early trustees appreciated financial support from the Presbyterian church and seem to have been determined to hire a Presbyterian pastor to lead the College. That happened in 1850, when Rev. John Adams Savage began a thirteen-year tenure as Carroll's first president.

The university's formal affiliation with the PCUSA (Presbyterian Church USA) has endured over the last 170 years, even as the lived experience of that identity has waxed and waned. For me, a historian by training, the *(in)sight* project offered an opportunity to reconsider what it might mean to profess a progressive religious affiliation in the 21st century. How does a largely unchurched generation of students understand Carroll's "Presbyterian heritage?"[26] What actions, values and relationships actualize the university's commitment "to make its student body aware of the Christian faith?"[27] Could *(in)sight* project interviews help us recognize, perhaps even revitalize, Carroll's own authentic institutional identity?[28]

By design, open-ended life history interviews recognize language and perception as powerful arbiters of collective identity. Because the process requires collaboration between interviewer and respondent, it fosters a sense of shared authority that explicitly recognizes the mutually-informing nature of individual & collective identity. For the *(in)sight* project, both interviewers and respondents affiliated with Carroll community. That shared identity, however, was just a starting point; it led to wide-ranging conversations that included not only introspection and vulnerability but also surprising parallels and laughter.

25 Ellen Langill, *Carroll College: The First Century* (Waukesha: Carroll College Press, 1980), 18.

26 Carroll University Mission Statement; Pew Research Center, "Trends in Religious Identity and Attendance" October 17, 2019 https://religioninpublic.blog/2020/02/10/generation-z-and-religion-what-new-data-show/ (accessed 12 June 2020)

27 Carroll University, Statement of Christian Purpose.

28 Political scientist Melissa Deckman's research seems to confirm this prediction, suggesting that today's college students are less likely to affiliate with a particular religious identity, while 45% say they "never or rarely" attend religious services. Melissa Deckman, "Generation Z and Religion: What New Data Show" blogpost Feb 10, 2020.

Drawing on the semi-structured 30-60 minute interviews, this essay explores *(in)sight* Project participants' perceptions of what they contribute to—and value in—the "special sauce" of the Carroll community.

First and foremost, the conversations reveal a surprising level of comfort with vulnerability. From nervous laughter, an exchange of names, and a request to "tell me something about yourself," structured dialogue quickly became rich, reflective conversations. Amanda Collette, for example, introduced herself as a caregiver:

> *For years I've babysat, but it's not the slightest bit as rewarding as being a caretaker… especially with a population that is so ostracized and so diminished in our society today… I do feel like the bridge between him and the rest of the world, so that he can experience things… I can share with him what goes on out there, things he can't see himself… I know that I can't reach… the entire disabled community, or people that are minorities, but I know that I am, I am making this boy happy and giving him opportunities that he wouldn't have had before. That's really all that matters to me.* [29]

Most of this interview revolves around Amanda's work with this client. It has helped her make sense of earlier struggles, including her parents' divorce and financial hardship, and has also articulated the lessons of other life experiences:

> *I've travelled the entire northern part of South America. So [I've seen] people don't want to be helped, but they want to know that there's someone out that that cares about them. So that's kind of my goal as a person, as my personality develops. I know that there hasn't been a lot of people out there that have stayed in my life, or made a super big impact on my life… I don't think people deserve that. They always deserve to have someone there for them… So I'm really passionate about nonprofits [and] social justice, especially with the immigrant community. That's a whole other conversation… I've been told for a long time by my boyfriend just to stop saying things and [to] start doing them. And it's really impacted me because, you know, I've always thought, "Why, oh why don't I be an activist or an advocate for someone?" But I don't really, I just don't want my voice to be heard; I want my actions to be understood. And you know, for there to be a purpose for what I'm doing.* [30]

---

29 Amanda Collette, "A bridge," interviewed by Emily Poffinbarger, April 2018.
30 Ibid.

Like Amanda, nearly all participants pondered the significance of some past difficulty or hurdle. Isabelle Banke. grew up with an aortic aneurysm, an invisible condition which nonetheless greatly limited her extracurricular activities. She had open heart surgery about six months before this conversation:

> When you look back, now, after surgery, I'm a totally different person. I feel like people think that I live a really hard life with all this, these limitations. But really, I think the hardest part was having to explain to people because I look fine; nothing looks wrong with me. The hardest part was, especially before I had surgery, I couldn't just pull up my shirt and be like, "Look there's a giant scar there." It's huge. You can't miss it (both laugh). Trying to explain to people that I really was sick. [Even teachers], all the time they'd say, "You look fine," and I'd be like, "I'm not fine" (laughs). So college has been great in that sense because I felt more normal than I have in a really long time.[31]

in(sight) participants also emphasize choice and deliberate action. Hannah Prosser, for example, recalls consciously choosing defiance when confronted with a potentially career-ending injury:

> I broke everything. And the doctors told me I should not dance again. And I was like, "Screw you, guys." ...I was determined to get back into it... The following year, they said never do en pointe again. They were firm on that. I was like, again, "Screw you." I was that kind of person, like I'll do what I want. So then a year after that I did an en pointe solo recital, just to prove it to myself that I can still do this if I want to... I did it and it was great. And then I never did en pointe after that, but I just had to prove it to myself. This is my life. If I don't do it, what's my point here?

Neither Isabelle nor Hannah allowed the external circumstances—the disease and accident, respectively—to have the final word. Isabelle notes, "I feel like open heart surgery proved, I proved to myself that I can pretty much do anything because I survived that shit."[32] Similarly, Hannah observes that it's not the car crash, but rather the proof of her own tenaciousness, that remains an important touchstone. Two and a half years after being told to stop dancing completely, she joined the Carroll dance team. Explaining her dream of performing with a NFL dance squad, she doesn't mince words:

> It's going to be rough. I'll audition next May. Starting in January, they have prep classes every single Friday until auditions, so I'll be taking all those, and then I also want to dance at other studios in the area... I'm, I'm totally planning on it to take me three times to even make it past the first stage.[33]

---

31 Isabelle Banke, "Invisible scars," interviewed by Katie Dobrzynski, April 2018.
32 Ibid.
33 Hannah Prosser, "This is my life," interviewed by Clara Clifford, April 2018.

Experienced educators know that one strength of liberal arts institutions is their ability to help students take appropriate risks and wrestle with uncertainty. Jon Gordon. highlighted the reciprocal nature of revealing interpersonal vulnerabilities.

...By the end of the semester, I'm going to know about your family, your boyfriend, any of these other things, and you're going to know about my past history. Most of my students can probably [name] two or three of my past girlfriends, and my brothers and sisters, and all of these things... That conversation has to happen. And if I want the student to share, I have to share.[34]

Third, *in(sight)* participants are grateful people. Asked about "the most important people in your life," participants often paused to reflect before, more often than not, identifying their mother. Shelby Stephan. explained what she most appreciates about her mom, a single parent of two:

She is very independent. She recently started dating this one guy, probably like four or five years ago. And he lives with us or whatever but, she—when she's mad at him you can tell... she really, she's so independent that she does not rely on him at all because she's used to being on her own for so long. And that makes me look up to her because mostly, I think most females... they feel like they need that man to lean on... You really don't— you can do it all by yourself without any help.[35]

Maggie Treants. was one of only a few exceptions to this pattern of recognizing maternal figures. Thinking about the source of her own resilience, she pointed to her father's influence.

My dad is the most important person in my life. One hundred percent. He's been through hell. I mean that; he's nearly died multiple times. He has M.S., but you'd never know, because he's the strongest person I know. [Doctors] were basically saying, "You're going to be paralyzed when you're 30." He does like martial arts and stuff now. He's crazy, I don't know how he does it. He takes care of our family and my grandma and all the stuff he's done in his life; he just keeps pushing... I have never met somebody with drive like that. And I just, I guess every time I feel like something is the end of the world for me—a really bad situation—I think about him and I'm like, "Ok, he got through. He got through, almost died; I can do it. I'll be fine.[36]

34 Jon Gordon, "Not a perfect science," interviewed by Ashley Labodda, April 2018.
35 Shelby Stephan, "Open mind, open heart," interviewed by Julia Nelson, April 2018.
36 Maggie Treants, "Get past your fear," interviewed by Alyssa Polewaczyk and Desirae Dunn, April 2018.

It's not surprising to see 19-24 year-olds express gratitude for parental figures. College takes many away from home for the first extended period of time; that distance opens opportunities for reflection. Interestingly, however, faculty and staff were also eager to talk about parental figures. Jim Gannon. mentioned the importance of peer friendships but quickly noted the formative role his grandfather played:

> *Grandpa taught me discipline, to be tough in a mental way. I mean, it's not like I was a bully, but tough. Don't let things stop you. Yeah, my grandfather taught me the importance of showing up, being disciplined, and not getting discouraged.[37]*

Participants' sense of gratitude is informed by their (re)interpretation of unforeseen circumstances. In other words, they see past difficulties as fueling contemporary tenacity and optimism. Nearly all, in fact, seemed to ground their goals in optimistic worldviews. Bethany K. dreamed of personalizing K-12 education through multi-modal interventions that "leave no one behind."[38] Zachary S. said simply, "In any job, working towards anything, it's leaving things better than I found it."[39] Greg G. expanded on this sentiment.

> *My wife says she doesn't want to be married to a congressman. I don't think I would necessarily win, but getting involved [in politics] in some way, just trying to figure out more ways to contribute to the greater good is important. I mean, I think I teach because I get to help make the world a little bit of a better place—or a less awful place. Whatever awful things are happening now are objectively true, but in a weird way, it's also better. I mean, when my grandma was born, women weren't allowed to vote! [I think] keeping the long view in mind is important.[40]*

Fourth, participants' responses, even to questions about personal values, almost never cited religious beliefs. When asked explicitly about spirituality, only Carl Erwin offered elaboration. "[My mother] always looks for the good in folks—God first, then family... She's always helping other folks, and I try to follow in her footsteps. [Dad] is more family first, and Mom is more God first..." Still, even Carl struggled to explain how his faith influenced his commitment to service. "It's just culture. [Growing up,] you learn, 'Well, that's how they're supposed to be' from day one; that's why you always remember where you're going."[41]

---

37 Jim Gannon, "Showing up," interviewed by Grace Egan, April 2018.
38 Bethany Kelly, "What hope looks like," interviewed by Claudia Splice, April 2018.
39 Zach Staszewski, "Alumni for Life," interviewed by Claire Pomey and Erin Sullivan, April 2018.
40 Greg Gabrielsen, "A huge gap," interviewed by Mia Pham, April 2018.
41 Ervin, interview; Indiana University Center for Postsecondary Research, "2019 National Survey of Student Engagement," 27, 37. This isn't especially surprising, given documented demographic trends. Still, for institution that asserts a denominational connection, it might be worth further study.

And the mythical "special sauce?" The value of campus community? Shelby Stephan noted "Coming [to Carroll] made me have more of an open mind, an open heart-type thing."[42] Greg Gabrielsen values "the fact that there's young people seeing things that they want to change and doing that."[43] Isabella Ruggiero added,I've learned a lot about relationship maintenance [at Carroll], so I see myself really making an effort to maintain contact with the people that are close to me and being very transparent… I want people to continue to build each other up instead of breaking each other down… to realize that they have to work together in order to get things done [and build]… toward a broader vision instead of just personal success.[44]

This focus on relationships included noting how other Pioneers have supported them. Tuna W. exemplifies this.

I'm basically a caregiver… When my mother was sick, I took care of her; when my dad was sick, I took care of him. And my husband [was] ill for a couple of years. So it was a lot of running back and forth. And at work… [My boss] let me come and go as I needed… [Looking back], I think I would keep even the mistakes and the heartbreak. It makes you a tougher person; it makes you someone who can empathize better. If you've never had a bad day, you're not going to know how somebody else feels.[45]

Tuna values her supervisor's flexibility but went a step further in her (in)sights conversation; that accommodation allowed her to be more authentic both as a caregiver and an employee. Student Thitikan Thianjan. voiced a similar thought comparing educational experiences in Thailand and the United States:

…Teachers over here, it's a lot more forgiving… They're really very helpful. They're like God's son (sic): they can help you with anything. [You have to] approach the people first to get to know them, rather than just ignore them… [That way] they know more of me and I more of them without faking it.[46]

42 Stephan, interview, April 2018.
43 Gabrielsen, interview, April 2018.
44 Isabella Ruggiero, "Build each other up," interviewed by Emma Kern, April 2018.
45 Tuna, Wallace. Tuna (Rosalie) Wallace, "No one is better than anybody else," interviewed by Casaundra Johnson, April 2018.
46 Thitikan Thianjan, "Expectations," interviewed by Corey Kowalski and Cassidy Neefe, April 2018.

Brandon Koster credited Carroll with challenging him—a kind of support that's more easily recognized after the fact:

> [I was] kind of shy and stifled my first couple years here at Carroll… I really appreciate [two professors for] making me a more outgoing person, a more creative person, and teaching me how to meld the academic part of my life with the creative part of my life. It was a big leap for me.[47]

Brandon learned from Carroll faculty that accepting complexity, difference or imperfection needn't be a passive response. Hannah Prosser. recognized this as well:"Being a [team] captain has taught me leadership skills, how to talk to people better, 'cause I feel like prior to this, my communication skills were kind of crappy. You have to be nice to your team, but you also have to be hard on them to be sure they're doing the right stuff."[48] Similarly, Czarina Encarnacion realized, "Something that I take away from being involved on campus is learning how to utilize my strengths and my weaknesses.[49] Isabella Ruggiero put this idea into a larger cultural context.

> I think the biggest lesson for me has been don't have expectations. In high school I had this picture of myself, what I wanted to do. I kind of had things planned out, and I just assumed they would happen. I mean even with coming to college, I thought I was going to go to this school in New York, and that didn't happen… I studied abroad my sophomore year of college. I'd always said I was going to go to Italy; I'm 50% Italian, I have family in Italy, I was going. No. Did not go to Italy. I studied in Vienna, Austria, which was fantastic, but again, I had this plan for myself, and that totally got washed away. [Or after] my grandma died… People started yelling at each other and not being nice to each other, to say the least…. American society kind of creates this idea that… if you're family, we love you no matter what, [but also] expectations of having this perfect family… That was the first time I really had insight into my mom and my aunt's childhood, and I realized that things aren't always perfect. [It] was really hard for me to see my mom struggling and to reconcile this with the perception I had of my grandma, because to me, she was great. That was really hard… it [shook] my world.[50]

---

47 Koster, interview.
48 Prosser, interview.
49 Czarina Encarnacion, "Just go with it," interviewed by Loey Dodge and Steven Grabowski, April 2018.
50 Ruggiero, interview.

We conceived the interview component of the *(in)sight* project as a way to "see" participants through another lens, i.e. as a complement to the work of the student and community artists. And on one level, the *(in)sight* interviews are just that—a co-sculpted portrait that captures some small part of a person and a life. Viewed collectively, however, the interviews also reveal core values of a community. These conversations show an aspirational collective identity with at least four common attributes:

1. An eagerness to reflect on circumstances and experiences, not for nostalgia's sake, but to gain and share wisdom.

2. A commitment to community service that springs from gratitude.

3. A person-to-person vision of both education and service as communal pursuits that promote individual integrity and autonomy.

4. An understanding of motivations—the "why" of one's actions—as a largely private, personal matter.

At 175 years, Carroll University, like institutions of higher ed across the country, faces demographic challenges. Meanwhile, the Presbyterian Church USA , like other major Christian denominations, is encountering financial constraints and a second generation of growing skepticism toward mainstream religious institutions. Interestingly, however, key tenets of the Presbyterian Church (i.e. of contemporary reformed theology) actually align with the insights noted above. For example, Presbyterian doctrine asserts that gratitude (not personal salvation) is the basis for public service, and that every individual must wrestle with questions of calling, purpose, and responsibility. The PCUSA asserts, furthermore, that no group or individual can know God's will for others.[51] In short, it confirms that our most meaningful truths, while often explored in community, are discerned at the individual level.

These ideas, expressed in multiple examples and diverse vocabularies, shine through the *(in)sight* project interviews. The conversations reveal more than the individual stories of well-known or much-respected members of the Carroll community. Like the sculpted and sketched portraits, each conversation offers a bridge between individual and institutional identities. At Carroll, evidence of Presbyterian heritage no longer takes the form of daily chapel or ordained leadership. Nonetheless, even Rev. Savage would recognize the commitment to what Thomas Johnson (class of 1860) described as "education in the highest sense," combining "the learning of the schools" and the enlightenment of the heart.[52]

—Kimberly A. Redding

---

51 Douglass, Jane Dempsey, "Predestination," interviewed by Vic Jameson, Presbyterian Mission Agency, u.d., https://www.presbyterianmission.org/what-we-believe/predestination/
52 Langill, 37.

References

Deckman, Melissa. "Generation Z and Religion: What New Data Show" Religion in Public (blog). February 10, 2020 https://religioninpublic.blog/2020/02/10/generation-z-and-religion-what-new-data-show/

Douglass, Jane Dempsey. "Predestination." By Vic Jameson Presbyterian Mission Agency, u.d. https://www.presbyterianmission.org/what-we-believe/predestination/

Center for Postsecondary Research. "2019 National Survey of Student Engagement." Bloomington, IN: Indiana University, 2019.

Langill, Ellen. Carroll College: The First Hundred Years. Waukesha: Carroll College, 1980.

Smith, Gregory A., et al. "In U.S., Decline of Christianity Continues at Rapid Pace" (report). Pew Research Center, October 17, 2019. https://www.pewforum.org/2019/10/17/in-u-s-decline-of-christianity-continues-at-rapid-pace/

A Special Thanks to:

The 175th Committee

Charlie Byler

Robert Colletta

Amy Cropper

Sara Meyer

Joanne Passaro

Cameron Tom

The Mary Nohls Fund

The Ten16 Press Team

All the artists, models and writers

And everyone who supported (in)sight: a portrait project

www.ingramcontent.com/pod-product-compliance
Lightning Source LLC
Chambersburg PA
CBHW041313180526
45172CB00004B/1082